SILENT CHINA

SILENT CHINA

SILENT CHINA
Selected Writings of
LU XUN

EDITED AND TRANSLATED BY

GLADYS YANG

OXFORD UNIVERSITY PRESS

LONDON   OXFORD   NEW YORK

1973

Oxford University Press

LONDON OXFORD NEW YORK

GLASGOW TORONTO MELBOURNE WELLINGTON

CAPE TOWN IBADAN NAIROBI DAR ES SALAAM LUSAKA ADDIS ABABA

DELHI BOMBAY CALCUTTA MADRAS KARACHI LAHORE DACCA

KUALA LUMPUR SINGAPORE HONG KONG TOKYO

ISBN 0 19 281150 9

Selection and Introduction
© Oxford University Press 1973

First published as an Oxford University Press paperback
by Oxford University Press, London, 1973

The translations by Gladys Yang of Lu Xun's writings are
from publications of the Foreign Languages Press, Peking.

*Printed in Great Britain by Richard Clay (The Chaucer Press), Ltd.,
Bungay, Suffolk.*

CONTENTS

INTRODUCTION

Lu Xun (Lu Hsun) is the great writer of modern China. His life spanned several decades of the prolonged revolution, led in its later stages by Mao Tsetung, that remade China. Dying in 1936, on the eve of the Sino-Japanese War, he did not see his country's liberation and emergence as a modern state. However, his writings reflect the trend of history, foretelling the Chinese people's choice of socialism and the resurgence of China as a great nation.

Lu Xun, whose real name was Zhou Shuren, was born in 1881 in Shaoxing, south of the Yangtse Valley. His grandfather held a minor official post, and his father was a scholar. In 1893 his grandfather was imprisoned on a charge of bribery, and the sharp decline in the family fortunes was accelerated by his father's long illness followed by his death in 1896. Lu Xun later classified himself as the son of a family which had come down in the world. He paid many visits to pawnshops while still a boy only 'half the height' of the pawnshop counter.

During his boyhood Lu Xun also spent some time with relatives in the country. Here he made friends with the villagers' children, saw something of the impoverishment of the countryside as China's natural economy was destroyed by capitalism, and developed a sympathy with the peasants that was to stay with him.

This was during the declining years of the Qing dynasty. Earlier in the century the once powerful and self-sufficient Chinese empire, outstripped by the capitalist countries of the West, had been forced to open up treaty ports and foreign settlements and grant foreigners extra-territorial rights. The corrupt Manchu government, with the backing of the imperialist powers, was able to crush revolts aimed at changing the political and social system. In all its long history the great Middle Kingdom had never been reduced to such straits. China had become the sick man of Asia, a 'dish of loose sand'.

Patriotic scholars sought for some means to make China independent and strong. As the traditional ideological weapons had failed, they borrowed the theories of the West, such as evolution, bourgeois republicanism, and democracy. Western-style schools were opened, and many students were sent to study abroad.

Lu Xun's education combined the traditional with the modern.

Confucian schooling in childhood gave him a good grounding in the Chinese classics. But his family had no money. So in 1898, at the age of eighteen, he entered one of the new institutions teaching Western science and technology, the Naval Academy in Nanking, a free, state-run school of naval engineering. The next year he transferred to the School of Railways and Mines. Upon his graduation in 1901, he was awarded a government scholarship for further study in Japan.

At Kobun College, Tokyo, where he first studied Japanese, he read voraciously in Western philosophy, political science, and literature. China's backwardness and low international status were brought home to him ever more keenly. He met Chinese political refugees in Japan and took his stand with the most radical of these, joining the Guangfuhui (Resurgence Society) which aimed at setting up a republic. He wrote a short poem at this time expressing grief over his country's oppression and vowed to sacrifice himself to the cause of China's regeneration.

In 1904 Lu Xun went to Sendai to study medicine, in the hope of later popularizing modern science and overcoming the old superstitions which, as he describes in his reminiscences, had cut short his father's life. However, in 1906 he saw a slide of the execution of a Chinese during the Russo-Japanese War, and was staggered by the apathy of the Chinese onlookers. To cure disease now seemed less important than to arouse his fellow-countrymen; and he felt that literature was the best tool for this purpose. Thus from the start his aim in writing was political: to awaken and enlighten the Chinese people. He wrote articles on progressive trends in culture and on the poetry of revolt, and translated stories from countries of eastern Europe under Tsarist rule, where conditions had much in common with those of China.

Lu Xun had originally intended to go to Germany for further study. In 1909, however, his younger brother Zhou Zuoren, who was also studying in Japan, married a Japanese wife, thus increasing the family's financial burden, and Lu Xun had to return to China to support his mother and two younger brothers.

Lu Xun's first job in China was teaching biology and chemistry in Chekiang Normal School, the teacher-training college in his native province. He then became dean of studies of a school in his home town. After the 1911 Revolution which established the Chinese Republic under Sun Yatsen, Lu Xun became the principal of Shaoxing Normal School. Early in 1912 he was invited to work in the Ministry of Education in Nanking, seat of the provisional government of the new Republic, and when the capital moved that same year to Peking, Lu Xun accompanied the ministry to the north.

The 1911 Revolution had toppled the Qing dynasty, but because it did not mobilize the people it failed to overcome the foreign and feudal domination of China. The old reactionary forces retained power, as Lu Xun describes in 'The True Story of Ah Q'. The ambitious ex-Manchu official Yuan Shikai ousted Sun Yatsen, made himself president, and in 1916 tried to restore the monarchy. Although he failed, power remained in the hands of northern militarist cliques. China was a republic in name only. In reality it was a semi-feudal, semi-colonial country fought over by contending warlords each of whom had the backing of a different foreign power.

Lu Xun was deeply disillusioned by the failure of the 1911 Revolution. For several years, while working in the Ministry of Education in Peking, he immersed himself in old books, studied Buddhist philosophy, and collected stone-rubbings. The Western school system, natural sciences, and social and political theories which he had helped to introduce had done much to discredit China's traditional ideology, but these had now been proved powerless in the face of the alliance between imperialist and feudal forces. What was the way out?

The answer for many Chinese intellectuals came with the October Revolution of 1917 and the establishment in Russia of the first socialist state. Chinese whose dreams of achieving a Western-style democracy had been shattered now saw in Russia a model for a more thoroughgoing revolution. In the cultural field this involved a revolution in the written language. The classical Chinese written by scholars was unintelligible to the common people, most of whom were illiterate; and if 'silent' China's millions were to be enlightened the written language had to be brought much closer to the vernacular. In 1918 Lu Xun began to write poems, short stories, and essays in colloquial Chinese. His story 'A Madman's Diary', an impassioned call to fight against the man-eating old culture, was published in April that year in *New Youth*, the most influential progressive journal of the day. He followed this up with the essay 'My Views on Chastity'. This was the real start of his literary career, and the time when he began using the pen-name Lu Xun.

In 1919 Lu Xun helped to launch the May Fourth Movement, which started as a student movement against imperialism and feudalism and gradually enlisted the support of wide sections of Chinese society. Among its slogans were: 'Down with the old ethics and up with the new!' 'Down with the old literature and up with the new!' Lu Xun through his writings acted as the standard-bearer of this movement, and did all he could to support the student vanguard. In 1920 he began lecturing at Peking University and other colleges. His influence on young intellectuals was growing, although many of his stories and prose poems of these years reveal a deep sense of personal isolation and anguish. But being Lu Xun, he never gave up fighting. In 1925 he championed the students of the Peking Women's Normal College who opposed their reactionary president. Later one of them, Xu Guangping, became his wife.

In March 1926, the Peking warlord government killed or wounded more than two hundred unarmed patriots, mostly students, for demonstrating against imperialism. Lu Xun, who spoke up for them, had to go into hiding. In August that year, to avoid persecution in Peking, he went south to Amoy University; but finding the place a stagnant backwater, he resigned at the end of the year. In January 1927 he accepted a post in the Sun Yatsen University in Canton, storm centre of the second democratic revolution.

Since 1924 the progressive wing of the Kuomintang Nationalists had been co-operating with the Communists to combat the northern warlords. In 1926 their joint forces set out from Canton on the Northern Expedition and within a few months had control of southern and central China. But Sun Yatsen had died by then, and his successor Chiang Kai-shek suddenly turned against the Communists and the Kuomintang's own left wing, and in April 1927 initiated a reign of white terror.

The years 1927–37 saw the first civil war between the Nationalists and the Communists. Chiang Kai-shek organized two series of 'encirclement and suppression' campaigns, military ones to wipe out the Communist base in the Jinggang Mountains of central China, and cultural ones to suppress democratic opinion. Both ended in failure. In 1934 the Red Army broke through encirclement and set out on the Long March, while popular demands for democracy steadily grew, drawing inspiration from Lu Xun's fearless polemical writings.

Lu Xun never joined the Communist Party, but during these stormy years he came to believe that Communist leadership was the only way to save China. In October 1927 he had moved to Shanghai, where the next year his only son was born, and where he remained till the time of his death. He studied and worked indefatigably. In 1928 he joined the Chinese Revolutionary Mutual-Aid Society. In 1930 he was a founding member of the China Freedom League and the China League of Left-Wing Writers. In 1933 he joined the China League for Civil Rights. A patriot and an internationalist, he opposed not only Chiang Kai-shek's fascist rule and Japanese aggression in

China, but was against all imperialist wars and strongly condemned Nazi persecution of the Jews.

The Kuomintang murdered progressive writers, and Lu Xun living under this reign of terror was often forced to go into hiding, as he writes in his poem 'Long Nights'. He had to resort to over a hundred different pen-names and to the use of innuendo and allusion to get his work passed by the censor. In his later years he gave up writing stories in favour of essays dealing with topical issues. Some of his friends deplored the fact that he spent so much time on ephemmeral political writing, but Lu Xun replied that his essays were daggers and darts hurled at the reactionaries to expose abuse and falsehood, and write them he must.

Lu Xun had hoped to collect material for a full-length novel about the epic Long March, but he died before this book could be written. At the end of 1935, when he heard that the Red Army had successfully reached the north-west, he sent a telegram of congratulations to the Central Committee of the Party in which he wrote: 'In you lies the hope of China and all humanity.' And when, in 1936, after Mao Tsetung called for a united front with Chiang Kai-shek against Japan, some Chinese Trotskyites accused the Communists of betraying the revolution,[1] Lu Xun stated his position explicitly: 'I count it an honour to have as my comrades those who are now doing solid work, treading firmly on the ground, fighting and shedding their blood in the defence of the Chinese people.'

In spite of ill health, persecution, and the pressure of work, Lu Xun gave generously of his time to help young writers and artists. Friends who knew him in the thirties recall him as a short, emaciated, haggard figure, well aware that his tuberculosis was incurable, but refusing to be hospitalized as long as he could stand up to fight. Striding along in his shabby old white silk gown, he retained his almost boyish exuberance and mordant sense of humour to the last. At a reception at the Russian Consulate in Shanghai to commemorate the October Revolution, Lu Xun's disreputable felt hat fell behind the hat-stand. When he retrieved it he kicked it down the stairs and pummelled it before putting it on. 'This is a rickshaw-puller's hat,' he said. 'And that's all I am—a rickshaw-puller.'

As he had written earlier:

> Fierce-browed I coolly defy a thousand pointing fingers.
> Head bowed, like a willing ox, I serve the children.

Lu Xun defied the reactionaries and worked for the people all his life. Mao Tsetung has called him 'The chief commander of China's

[1] See below, pp. 187–9.

cultural revolution . . . not only a great man of letters but a great thinker and revolutionary'; and elsewhere, 'the bravest and most correct, the firmest, the most loyal and the most ardent national hero, a hero without parallel in our history'.

As the dates at the end of the selections indicate, Lu Xun's writings were originally published in magazines and newspaper supplements, 'The True Story of Ah Q' appearing as a serial. The majority of his stories and reminiscences, including the first four stories in this selection, were written between 1918 and 1926. After 1927, polemical articles and essays formed his main output, but in addition he wrote some historical tales with a topical significance such as 'Leaving the Pass', written in 1935. Besides two collections of short stories, one of *Old Tales Retold*, a volume of prose poems, one of reminiscences, and over 600 essays, Lu Xun wrote a history of Chinese fiction, made many translations of foreign literature and literary criticism, and edited and published albums of Chinese and foreign art. He also left diaries and a large number of letters to friends and to his wife.

To make a selection from all this wealth of material is difficult. I have tried to indicate something of Lu Xun's versatility, the causes he championed and the abuses he attacked; but considerations of space and the difficulty of understanding certain of his writings without a knowledge of their historical background, have forced me to omit many important works—the essays dealing with the relationship between literature and revolution, for instance. Lu Xun's brilliant writing in the vernacular helped to shape modern Chinese prose, and I have included a number of prose poems written in the vernacular, as well as poems in the classical style.

The List of Sources at p. 195, compiled by W. J. F. Jenner, gives the Chinese volume from which each of the selections is taken. Mr. Jenner has also provided the Note on Pronunciation at p. 196, for Chinese names which are romanized in this volume according to the Hanyu Pinyin system. This book owes much to his assistance and advice. I am also very grateful to Miss Catharine Carver of the Oxford University Press for her expert and understanding editorial help in the later stages of preparing this book.

Most of the writings in this selection are revised versions of translations from the 1957 edition of *Lu Xun quan ji* done with the help of my husband and published by the Foreign Languages Press, Peking. I am grateful for the permission to use this material and am alone responsible for any errors in the new versions.

Peking, 1973   GLADYS YANG

Stories

Stories

A Madman's Diary 狂 人 日 记

Two brothers, whose names I need not mention here, were both good friends of mine in high school; but after a separation of many years we gradually lost touch. Some time ago I happened to hear that one of them was seriously ill, and since I was going back to my old home I broke my journey to call on them. I saw only one, however, who told me that the invalid was his younger brother.

'I appreciate your coming such a long way to see us,' he said, 'but my brother recovered some time ago and has gone elsewhere to take up an official post.' Then, laughing, he produced two volumes of his brother's diary, saying that from these the nature of his past illness could be seen and there was no harm in showing them to an old friend. I took the diary away, read it through, and found that he had suffered from a form of persecution complex. The writing was most confused and incoherent, and he had made many wild statements; moreover he had omitted to give any dates, so that only by the colour of the ink and the differences in the writing could one tell that it was not all written at one time. Certain sections, however, were not altogether disconnected, and I have copied out a part to serve as a subject for medical research. I have not altered a single illogicality in the diary and have changed only the names, even though the people referred to are all country folk, unknown to the world and of no consequence. As for the title, it was chosen by the diarist himself after his recovery, and I did not change it.

I

Tonight the moon is very bright.

I have not seen it for over thirty years, so today when I saw it I felt in unusually high spirits. I begin to realize that during the past thirty-odd years I have been in the dark; but now I must be extremely careful. Otherwise why should the Zhaos' dog have looked at me twice?

I have reason for my fear.

2

Tonight there is no moon at all, I know that this is a bad omen. This morning when I went out cautiously, Mr. Zhao had a strange look in his eyes, as if he were afraid of me, as if he wanted to murder me. There were seven or eight others who discussed me in a whisper. And they were afraid of my seeing them. So, indeed, were all the people I passed. The fiercest among them grinned at me; whereupon I shivered from head to foot, knowing that their preparations were complete.

I was not afraid, however, but continued on my way. A group of children in front were also discussing me, and the look in their eyes was just like that in Mr. Zhao's while their faces too were ghastly pale. I wondered what grudge these children could have against me to make them behave like this. I could not help calling out: 'Tell me!' But then they ran away.

I wonder what grudge Mr. Zhao has against me, what grudge the people on the road have against me. I can think of nothing except that twenty years ago I trod on Mr. Gu Jiu's[1] old ledgers, and Mr. Gu was most displeased. Although Mr. Zhao does not know him, he must have heard talk of this and decided to avenge him, thus he is conspiring against me with the people on the road. But then what of the children? At that time they were not yet born, so why should they eye me so strangely today, as if they were afraid of me, as if they wanted to murder me? This really frightens me, it is so bewildering and upsetting.

I know. They must have learned this from their parents!

[1] *Gu jiu* means 'ancient times'. Lu Xun had in mind the long history of feudal oppression in China.

3

I can't sleep at night. Everything requires careful consideration if one is to understand it.

Those people, some of whom have been pilloried by the magistrate, slapped in the face by the local gentry, had their wives taken away by bailiffs or their parents driven to suicide by creditors, never looked as frightened and as fierce then as they did yesterday.

The most extraordinary thing was that woman on the street yesterday who was spanking her son. 'Little devil!' she cried. 'I'm so angry I could eat you!' Yet all the time it was me she was looking at. I gave a start, unable to hide my alarm. Then all those long-toothed people with livid faces began to hoot with laughter. Old Chen hurried forward and dragged me home.

He dragged me home. The folk at home all pretended not to know me; they had the same look in their eyes as all the others. When I went into the study, they locked me in as if cooping up a chicken or a duck. This incident left me even more bewildered.

A few days ago a tenant of ours from Wolf Cub Village came to report the failure of the crops and told my elder brother that a notorious character in their village had been beaten to death; then some people had taken out his heart and liver, fried them in oil, and eaten them as a means of increasing their courage. When I interrupted, the tenant and my brother both stared at me. Only today have I realized that they had exactly the same look in their eyes as those people outside.

Just to think of it sets me shivering from the crown of my head to the soles of my feet.

They eat human beings, so they may eat me.

I see that the woman's 'eat you', the laughter of those long-toothed people with livid faces, and the tenant's story the other day are obviously secret signs. I realize all the poison in their speech, all the daggers in their laughter. Their teeth are white and glistening: they use these teeth to eat men.

Evidently, although I am not a bad man, ever since I trod on Mr. Gu's ledgers it has been touch-and-go with me. They seem to have secrets which I cannot guess, and once they are angry they will call anyone a bad character. I remember when my elder brother taught me to write compositions, no matter how good a man was, if I produced arguments to the contrary he would mark that passage to show his approval; while if I excused evil-doers he would say: 'Good for you, that shows originality.' How can I possibly guess their secret thoughts— especially when they are ready to eat people?

Everything requires careful consideration if one is to understand it. In ancient times, as I recollect, people often ate human beings, but I am rather hazy about it. I tried to look this up, but my history has no chronology and scrawled all over each page are the words: 'Virtue and Morality'. Since I could not sleep anyway, I read intently half the night until I began to see words between the lines. The whole book was filled with the two words—'Eat people.'

All these words written in the book, all the words spoken by our tenant, eye me quizzically with an enigmatic smile.

I too am a man, and they want to eat me!

4

In the morning I sat quietly for some time. Old Chen brought in lunch: one bowl of vegetables, one bowl of steamed fish. The eyes of the fish were white and hard, and its mouth was open just like those people who want to eat human beings. After a few mouthfuls I could not tell whether the slippery morsels were fish or human flesh, so I brought it all up.

I said, 'Old Chen, tell my brother that I feel quite suffocated and want to have a stroll in the garden.' Old Chen said nothing but went out, and presently he came back and opened the gate.

I did not move, but watched to see how they would treat me, feeling certain that they would not let me go. Sure enough! My elder brother came slowly out, leading an old man. There was a murderous gleam in his eyes, and fearing that I would see it he lowered his head, stealing side-glances at me from behind his glasses.

'You seem very well today,' said my brother.

'Yes,' said I.

'I have invited Mr. He here today to examine you.'

'All right,' I replied. Actually I knew quite well that this old man was the executioner in disguise! Feeling my pulse was simply a pretext for him to see how fat I was; for this would entitle him to a share of my flesh. Still I was not afraid. Although I do not eat men my courage is greater than theirs. I held out my two fists to see what he would do. The old man sat down, closed his eyes, fumbled for some time, remained motionless for a while; then opened his shifty eyes and said, 'Don't let your imagination run away with you. Rest quietly for a few days, and you will be better.'

Don't let your imagination run away with you! Rest quietly for a few days! By fattening me of course they'll have more to eat. But what good will it do me? How can it be 'better'? The whole lot of them wanting to eat people yet stealthily trying to keep up appearances, not daring to do it outright, was really enough to make me die of laughter. I couldn't help it, I nearly split my sides, I was so amused. I knew that this laughter voiced courage and integrity. Both the old man and my brother turned pale, awed by my courage and integrity.

But my courage just makes them all the more eager to eat me, to acquire some of my courage for themselves. The old man went out of the gate, but before he had gone far he said to my brother in a low voice, 'To be eaten at once!' My brother nodded. So you are in it too! This stupendous discovery, though it came as a shock, is no more than I might expect: the accomplice in eating me is my elder brother!

The eater of human flesh is my elder brother!

I am the younger brother of an eater of human flesh!

I, who will be eaten by others, am the younger brother of an eater of human flesh!

5

These few days I have been thinking again: suppose that old man were not an executioner in disguise, but a real doctor; he would be none the less an eater of human flesh. That book on herbs by his predecessor Li Shizhen [1] states explicitly that men's flesh can be boiled and eaten; how then can he still deny that he eats men?

[1] Famous pharmacologist (1518–93), author of *Materia Medica*.

As for my elder brother, I have also good reason to suspect him. When he was teaching me, he told me himself, 'People exchange their sons to eat.' And once in discussing a bad man he said that not only did the fellow deserve to be killed, he should 'have his flesh eaten and his hide slept on'.[1] I was still young at the time, and for quite a while my heart beat faster. That story our tenant from Wolf Cub Village told the other day about eating a man's heart and liver didn't surprise him at all—he kept nodding his head. He is evidently just as cruel as before. Since it is possible to 'exchange sons to eat', then anything can be exchanged, anyone can be eaten. In the past I simply listened to his explanations and let it go at that; now I know that when he gave me these explanations, not only was there human fat at the corner of his lips, but his whole heart was set on eating men.

6

Pitch dark. I don't know whether it is day or night. The Zhaos' dog has started barking again.

The fierceness of a lion, the timidity of a rabbit, the craftiness of a fox . .

7

I know their way: they are not prepared to kill outright, nor would they dare, for fear of the consequences. Instead they have banded together and set traps everywhere, to force me to kill myself. The behaviour of the men and women in the street a few days ago and my elder brother's attitude these last few days make it quite obvious. What they like best is for a man to take off his belt and hang himself from a beam; for then they can enjoy their hearts' desire without being blamed for murder. Naturally that delights them and sets them roaring with laughter. On the other hand, if a man is frightened or worried to death, though that makes him rather thin, they still nod in approval.

They only eat dead flesh! I remember reading somewhere of a

[1] These are quotations from the old classic *Zuo Zhuan*.

hideous beast with an ugly look in its eye called 'hyena', which often eats dead flesh. Even the largest bones it crunches into fragments and swallows; the mere thought of this makes your hair stand on end. Hyenas are related to wolves, wolves belong to the canine species. The other day the Zhaos' dog eyed me several times: it is obviously in the plot too as their accomplice. The old man's eyes were cast down, but that did not deceive me.

The most deplorable is my elder brother. He's a man too, so why isn't he afraid, why is he plotting with others to eat me? Does force of habit blind a man to what's wrong? Or is he so heartless that he will knowingly commit a crime?

In cursing man-eaters, I shall start with my brother. In dissuading man-eaters, I shall start with him too.

8

Actually such arguments should have convinced them long ago . . .

Suddenly someone came in. He was only about twenty years old and I did not see his features very clearly. His face was wreathed in smiles, but when he nodded to me his smile didn't seem genuine. I asked him: 'Is it right to eat human beings?'

Still smiling, he replied: 'When there is no famine how can one eat human beings?'

I realized at once he was one of them; but still I summoned up courage to repeat my question:

'Is it right?'

'What makes you ask such a thing? You really are . . . fond of a joke. . . . It is very fine today.'

'It is fine, and the moon is very bright. But I want to ask you: Is it right?'

He looked disconcerted and muttered: 'No . . .'

'No? Then why do they still do it?'

'What are you talking about?'

'What am I talking about? They are eating men now in Wolf Cub Village, and you can see it written all over the books, in fresh red ink.'

His expression changed. He grew ghastly pale. 'It may be so,' he said staring at me. 'That's the way it's always been. . . .'

'Does that make it right?'

'I refuse to discuss it with you. Anyway, you shouldn't talk about it. It's wrong for anyone to talk about it.'

I leaped up and opened my eyes wide, but the man had vanished. I was soaked with sweat. He was much younger than my elder brother, but even so he was in it. He must have been taught by his parents. And I am afraid he has already taught his son; that is why even the children look at me so fiercely.

9

Wanting to eat men, at the same time afraid of being eaten themselves, they all eye each other with the deepest suspicion. . . .

How comfortable life would be for them if they could rid themselves of such obsessions and go to work, walk, eat, and sleep at ease. They have only this one step to take. Yet fathers and sons, husbands and wives, brothers, friends, teachers and students, sworn enemies and even strangers, have all joined in this conspiracy, discouraging and preventing each other from taking this step.

10

Early this morning I went to find my elder brother. He was standing outside the hall door looking at the sky when I walked up behind him, standing between him and the door, and addressed him with exceptional poise and politeness:

'Brother, I have something to say to you.'

'Go ahead then.' He turned quickly towards me, nodding.

'It's nothing much, but I find it hard to say. Brother, probably all primitive people ate a little human flesh to begin with. Later, because their views altered some of them stopped and tried so hard to do what was right that they changed into men, into real men. But some are still eating people—just like reptiles. Some have changed into fish, birds, monkeys, and finally men; but those who make no effort to do what's right are still reptiles. When those who eat men compare themselves with those who don't, how ashamed they must be. Probably much more ashamed than the reptiles are before monkeys.

'In ancient times Yi Ya boiled his son for Jie and Zhou to eat; that is the old story. But actually since the creation of heaven and earth by Pan Gu men have been eating each other, from the time of Yi Ya's son to the time of Xu Xilin,[1] and from the time of Xu Xilin down to the man caught in Wolf Cub Village. Last year they executed a criminal in the city, and a consumptive soaked a piece of bread in his blood and sucked it.

'They want to eat me, and of course you can do nothing about it single-handed; but why must you join them? As man-eaters they are capable of anything. If they eat me, they can eat you as well; members of the same group can still eat each other. But if you will just change your ways, change right away, then everyone will have peace. Although this has been going on since time immemorial, today we could make a special effort to do what is right, and say this can't be done! I'm sure you can say that, brother. The other day when the tenant wanted the rent reduced, you said it couldn't be done.'

At first he only smiled cynically, then a murderous gleam came into his eyes, and when I spoke of their secret he turned pale. Outside the gate quite a crowd had gathered, among them Mr. Zhao and his dog, all craning their necks to peer in. I could not see all their faces, some of them seemed to be masked; others were the old lot, long-toothed with livid faces, concealing their laughter. I knew they were one gang, all eaters of human flesh. But I also knew that they did not all think alike by any means. Some of them thought that since it had always been so, men should be eaten. Others knew they shouldn't eat men but still wanted to, and were afraid people might discover their secret; so although what I said made them angry they still smiled their cynical, tight-lipped smiles.

Suddenly my brother's face darkened.

'Clear off, the whole lot of you!' he roared. 'What's the point of looking at a madman?'

Then I realized part of their cunning. They would never be

[1] A revolutionary executed in 1907 for assassinating a Qing official. His heart and liver were eaten.

willing to change their stand, and their plans were all laid: they
had labelled me a madman. In future when I was eaten, not
only would there be no trouble but people would probably be
grateful to them. When our tenant spoke of the villagers eating
a bad character, it was exactly the same device. This is their
old trick.

Old Chen came in too in a towering temper. But they could
not stop my mouth, I had to warn those people:

'You should change, change from the bottom of your hearts.
You must realize that there will be no place for man-eaters
in the world in future.

'If you don't change, you may all be eaten by each other.
However many of you there are, you will be wiped out by the
real men, just as wolves are killed by hunters—just like reptiles!'

Old Chen drove everybody away. My brother had disappeared. Old Chen advised me to go back to my room. It was
pitch dark in there. The beams and rafters shook above my
head. After shaking for a while they grew bigger and bigger.
They piled on top of me.

The weight was so great, I couldn't move. They meant that I
should die. However, knowing that the weight was false I
struggled out, dripping with sweat. But I had to warn them:

'You must change at once, change from the bottom of your
hearts! You must know that there'll be no place for man-eaters
in future. . . .'

II

The sun has stopped shining, the door is never opened. Just
two meals day after day.

Picking up my chopsticks, I thought of my elder brother. I
know now how my little sister died: it was all through him.
My sister was only five at the time. I can still remember how
sweet she looked, poor thing. Mother wept as if she would
never stop, but he begged her not to cry, probably because he
had eaten our sister himself and so this weeping made him
rather ashamed. If he had any sense of shame . . .

My sister was eaten by my brother, but I don't know whether
Mother realized it or not.

I think Mother must have known, but when she wept she didn't say so outright, probably because she also thought it proper. I remember when I was four or five, sitting in the cool of the hall, my brother told me that if a man's parents were ill he should cut off a piece of his flesh and boil it for them, if he wanted to be considered a good son; and Mother didn't contradict him. If one piece could be eaten, obviously so could the whole. And yet just to think of the weeping then still makes my heart bleed; that is the extraordinary thing about it!

12

I can't bear to think of it.

It has only just dawned on me that all these years I have been living in a place where for four thousand years human flesh has been eaten. My brother had just taken over the charge of the house when our sister died, and he may well have used her flesh in our food, making us eat it unwittingly.

I may have eaten several pieces of my sister's flesh unwittingly, and now it is my turn. . . .

How can a man like myself, after four thousand years of man-eating history—even though I knew nothing about it at first—ever hope to face real men?

♦

13

Perhaps there are still children who haven't eaten men.

Save the children. . . .

2 April 1918

The True Story of Ah Q   阿 Q 正 传

CHAPTER 1

Introduction

For several years now I have been meaning to write the true story of Ah Q. But while wanting to write I was in some trepidation too, which goes to show that I am not one of those who achieve glory by writing; for an immortal pen has always been required to record the deeds of an immortal man, the man becoming known to posterity through the writing and the writing known to posterity through the man—until finally it is not clear who is making whom known. But in the end, as though possessed by some fiend, I always came back to the idea of writing the story of Ah Q.

And yet no sooner had I taken up my pen than I became conscious of tremendous difficulties in writing this far-from-immortal work. The first was the question of what to call it. Confucius said, 'If the name is not correct, the words will not ring true'; and this axiom should be most scrupulously observed. There are many types of biography: official biographies, autobiographies, unauthorized biographies, legends, supplementary biographies, family histories, sketches . . . but unfortunately none of these suited my purpose. 'Official biography'? This account will obviously not be included with those of many eminent people in some authentic history. 'Autobiography'? But I am obviously not Ah Q. If I were to call this an 'unauthorized biography', then where is his 'authenticated biography'? The use of 'legend' is impossible because Ah Q was no legendary figure. 'Supplementary biography'? But no president has ever ordered the National Historical Institute to write a 'standard life' of Ah Q. It is true that although there are no 'lives of gamblers' in authentic English history, the well-known author Conan Doyle never-

theless wrote *Rodney Stone*;[1] but while this is permissible for a
well-known author it is not permissible for such as I. Then there
is 'family history'; but I do not know whether I belong to the
same family as Ah Q or not, nor have his children or grand-
children ever entrusted me with such a task. If I were to use
'sketch', it might be objected that Ah Q has no 'complete
account'. In short, this is really a 'life', but since I write in
vulgar vein using the language of hucksters and pedlars, I dare
not presume to give it so high-sounding a title. So I will take as
my title the last two words of a stock phrase of the novelists, who
are not reckoned among the Three Cults and Nine Schools,[2]
'Enough of this digression, and back to the *true story*'; and if this
is reminiscent of the *True Story of Calligraphy*[3] of the ancients, it
cannot be helped.

The second difficulty confronting me was that a biography
of this type should start off something like this: 'So-and-so,
whose other name was so-and-so, was a native of such-and-such
a place'; but I don't really know what Ah Q's surname was.
Once, he seemed to be named Zhao, but the next day there was
some confusion about the matter again. This was after Mr.
Zhao's son had passed the county examination and, to the sound
of gongs, his success was announced in the village. Ah Q, who
had just drunk two bowls of yellow wine, began to prance
about declaring that this reflected credit on him too, since he
belonged to the same clan as Mr. Zhao and by an exact
reckoning was three generations senior to the successful
candidate. At the time several bystanders even began to stand
slightly in awe of Ah Q. But the next day the bailiff summoned
him to Mr. Zhao's house. When the old gentleman set eyes on
him his face turned crimson with fury and he roared:

'Ah Q, you miserable wretch! Did you say I belonged to
the same clan as you?'

Ah Q made no reply.

The more he looked at him the angrier Mr. Zhao became.
Advancing menacingly a few steps he said, 'How dare you talk

---

[1] In Chinese this title was translated as *Supplementary Biographies of the Gamblers*.
[2] The Three Cults were Confucianism, Buddhism, and Taoism. The Nine
Schools included the Confucian, Taoist, Legalist, Moist, and other schools.
[3] A book by Feng Wu of the Qing dynasty (1644–1911).

such nonsense! How could I have such a relative as you? Is your surname Zhao?'

Ah Q made no reply and was planning a retreat, when Mr. Zhao darted forward and gave him a slap on the face.

'How could *you* be named Zhao? Are you worthy of the name Zhao?'

Ah Q made no attempt to defend his right to the name Zhao but rubbing his left cheek went out with the bailiff from whom, once outside, he had to listen to another torrent of abuse. He then by way of atonement paid him two hundred cash. All who heard this said Ah Q was a great fool to ask for a beating like that. Even if his surname *were* Zhao—which wasn't likely—he should have known better than to boast like that when there was a Mr. Zhao living in the village. After this no further mention was made of Ah Q's ancestry, thus I still have no idea what his surname really was.

The third difficulty I encountered in writing this work was that I don't know how Ah Q's personal name should be written either. During his lifetime everybody called him Ah Quei,[1] but after his death not a soul mentioned Ah Quei again; for he was obviously not one of those whose name is 'preserved on bamboo tablets and silk'.[2] If there is any question of preserving his name, this essay must be the first attempt at doing so. Hence I am confronted with this difficulty at the outset. I have given the question careful thought. Ah Quei—would that be the 'Quei' meaning fragrant oleander or the 'Quei' meaning nobility? If his other name had been Moon Pavilion, or if he had celebrated his birthday in the month of the Moon Festival, then it would certainly be the 'Quei' for fragrant oleander.[3] But since he had no other name—or if he had, no one knew it—and since he never sent out invitations on his birthday to secure complimentary verses, it would be arbitrary to write Ah Quei (fragrant oleander). Again, if he had had an elder or younger brother called Ah Fu (prosperity), then he would certainly be called Ah Quei (nobility). But he was all on his own; thus there

[1] Lu Xun's romanized version of the character *gui*.
[2] A phrase used before paper was invented when bamboo and silk served as writing material in China.
[3] The fragrant oleander blooms in the month of the Moon Festival. And according to Chinese folklore, the shadow on the moon is an oleander tree.

is no justification for writing Ah Quei (nobility). All the other, unusual characters with the sound *quei* are even less suitable. I once put this question to Mr. Zhao's son, the successful county candidate, but even such a learned man as he was baffled by it. According to him, however, the reason why this name could not be traced was that Chen Duxiu had brought out the magazine *New Youth* advocating the use of the Western alphabet, hence the national culture was going to the dogs. As a last resort, I asked someone from my district to go and look up the legal documents recording Ah Q's case, but after eight months he sent me a letter saying that there was no name anything like Ah Quei in those records. Although uncertain whether this was the truth or whether my friend had simply done nothing, after failing to trace the name this way I could think of no other means of finding it. Since I am afraid the new system of phonetics has not yet come into common use, there is nothing for it but to use the Western alphabet, writing the name according to the English spelling as Ah Quei and abbreviating it to Ah Q. This approximates to blindly following *New Youth*, and I am thoroughly ashamed of myself; but since even such a learned man as Mr. Zhao's son could not solve my problem, what else can I do?

My fourth difficulty was with Ah Q's place of origin. If his surname were Zhao, then according to the old custom which still prevails of classifying people by their district, one might look up the commentary in *The Hundred Surnames*[1] and find 'Native of Tianshui in Longxi'. But unfortunately this surname is open to question, with the result that Ah Q's place of origin must also remain uncertain. Although he lived for the most part in Weizhuang, he often stayed in other places, so that it would be wrong to call him a native of Weizhuang. It would, in fact, amount to a distortion of history.

The only thing that consoles me is the fact that the character 'Ah' is absolutely correct. This is definitely not the result of false analogy, and is well able to stand the test of scholarly criticism. As for the other problems, it is not for such unlearned people as myself to solve them, and I can only hope that disciples of Dr. Hu Shi, who has such 'a passion for history and

[1] A school primer in which surnames were written into verse.

research', may be able in future to throw new light on them. I am afraid, however, that by that time my *True Story of Ah Q* will have long since passed into oblivion.

The foregoing may be considered as an introduction.

CHAPTER 2

A Brief Account of Ah Q's Victories

In addition to the uncertainty regarding Ah Q's surname, personal name, and place of origin, there is even some uncertainty regarding his 'background'. This is because the people of Weizhuang only made use of his services or treated him as a laughing-stock, without ever paying the slightest attention to his 'background'. Ah Q himself remained silent on this subject, except that when quarrelling with someone he might glare at him and say, 'We used to be much better off than you! Who do you think you are?'

Ah Q had no family but lived in the Tutelary God's Temple at Weizhuang. He had no regular work either, being simply an odd-job man for others: when there was wheat to be cut he would cut it, when there was rice to be hulled he would hull it, when there was a boat to be punted he would punt it. If the work lasted for any length of time he might stay in the house of his temporary employer, but as soon as it was finished he would leave. Thus whenever people had work to be done they would remember Ah Q, but what they remembered was his service and not his 'background'. By the time the job was done even Ah Q himself was forgotten, to say nothing of his 'background'. Once indeed an old man remarked, 'What a worker Ah Q is!' Ah Q, bare-backed scrawny sluggard, was standing before him at the time, and others could not tell whether the remark was serious or derisive, but Ah Q was overjoyed.

Ah Q, again, had a very high opinion of himself. He looked down on all the inhabitants of Weizhuang, thinking even the two young 'scholars' not worth a smile, though most young scholars were likely to pass the official examinations. Mr. Zhao and Mr. Qian were held in great respect by the villagers, for in addition to being rich they were both the fathers of young scholars. Ah Q alone showed them no exceptional deference, thinking to himself, 'My sons may be much greater.'

Moreover, after Ah Q had been to town several times he naturally became even more conceited, although at the same time he had the greatest contempt for townspeople. For instance, a bench made of a wooden plank three feet by three inches the Weizhuang villagers called a 'long bench'. Ah Q called it a 'long bench' too; but the townspeople called it a 'straight bench', and he thought, 'This is wrong. Ridiculous!' Again, when they fried large-headed fish in oil the Weizhuang villagers all added shallots sliced half an inch thick, whereas the townspeople added finely shredded shallots, and he thought, 'This is wrong too. Ridiculous!' But the Weizhuang villagers were really ignorant rustics who had never seen fish fried in town.

Ah Q who 'used to be much better off', who was a man of the world and a 'worker', would have been almost the perfect man had it not been for a few unfortunate physical blemishes. The most annoying were some patches on his scalp where at some uncertain date shiny ringworm scars had appeared. Although these were on his own head, apparently Ah Q did not consider them as altogether honourable, for he refrained from using the word 'ringworm' or any words that sounded anything like it. Later he improved on this, making 'bright' and 'light' forbidden words, while later still even 'lamp' and 'candle' were taboo. Whenever this taboo was disregarded, whether intentionally or not, Ah Q would fly into a rage, his ringworm scars turning scarlet. He would look over the offender, and if it were someone weak in repartee he would curse him, while if it were a poor fighter he would hit him. Yet, curiously enough, it was usually Ah Q who was worsted in these encounters, until finally he adopted new tactics, contenting himself in general with a furious glare.

It so happened, however, that after Ah Q had taken to using this furious glare, the idlers in Weizhuang grew even more fond of making jokes at his expense. As soon as they saw him they would pretend to give a start and say:

'Look! It's lighting up.'

Ah Q rising to the bait as usual would glare in fury.

'So there is a paraffin lamp here,' they would continue, unafraid.

Ah Q could do nothing but rack his brains for some retort. 'You don't even deserve . . .' At this juncture it seemed as if the bald patches on his scalp were noble and honourable, not just ordinary ringworm scars. However, as we said above, Ah Q was a man of the world: he knew at once that he had nearly broken the 'taboo' and refrained from saying any more.

If the idlers were still not satisfied but continued to pester him, they would in the end come to blows. Then only after Ah Q had to all appearances been defeated, had his brownish queue pulled and his head bumped against the wall four or five times, would the idlers walk away, satisfied at having won. And Ah Q would stand there for a second thinking to himself, 'It's as if I were beaten by my son. What is the world coming to nowadays. . . .' Thereupon he too would walk away, satisfied at having won.

Whatever Ah Q thought he was sure to tell people later; thus almost all who made fun of Ah Q knew that he had this means of winning a psychological victory. So after this anyone who pulled or twisted his brown queue would forestall him by saying: 'Ah Q, this is not a son beating his father, it is a man beating a beast. Let's hear you say it: A man beating a beast!'

Then Ah Q, clutching at the root of his queue, his head on one side, would say: 'Beating an insect—how about that? I am an insect—now will you let me go?'

But although he was an insect the idlers would not let him go until they had knocked his head five or six times against something nearby, according to their custom, after which they would walk away satisfied that they had won, confident that this time Ah Q was done for. In less than ten seconds, however, Ah Q would walk away also satisfied that he had won, thinking that he was the 'Number One self-belittler', and that after subtracting 'self-belittler' what remained was 'Number One'. Was not the highest successful candidate in the official examination also 'Number One'? 'And who do you think *you* are?'

After employing such cunning devices to get even with his enemies, Ah Q would make his way cheerfully to the tavern to drink a few bowls of wine, joke with the others again, quarrel with them again, come off victorious again, and return cheerfully to the Tutelary God's Temple, there to fall asleep as soon as his head touched the pillow. If he had money he would gamble. A group of men would squat on the ground, Ah Q sandwiched in their midst, his face streaming with sweat; and his voice would shout the loudest: 'Four hundred on the Green Dragon!'

'Hey—open there!'

The stake-holder, his face streaming with sweat too, would open the box and chant: 'Heavenly Gate!—Nothing for the Corner! . . . No stakes on Popularity Passage! Pass over Ah Q's coppers!'

'The Passage—one hundred—one hundred and fifty.'

To the tune of this chanting, Ah Q's money would gradually vanish into the pockets of other sweating players. Finally he would be forced to squeeze his way out of the crowd and watch from the back, taking a vicarious interest in the game until it broke up, when he would return reluctantly to the Tutelary God's Temple. The next day he would go to work with swollen eyes.

However, the truth of the proverb 'Misfortune may prove a blessing in disguise' was shown when Ah Q was unfortunate enough to win and almost suffered defeat in the end.

This was the evening of the Festival of the Gods in Weizhuang. According to custom there was an opera; and close to the stage, also according to custom, were numerous gambling tables. The drums and gongs of the opera sounded miles away to Ah Q who had ears only for the stake-holder's chant. He staked successfully again and again, his coppers turning into silver coins, his silver coins into dollars, and his dollars mounting up. In his excitement he cried out, 'Two dollars on Heavenly Gate!'

He never knew who started the fight, nor for what reason. Curses, blows, and footsteps formed a confused medley of sound in his head, and by the time he clambered to his feet the gambling tables had vanished and so had the gamblers. Several parts of his body seemed to be aching as if he had been kicked and knocked about, while a number of people were looking at him in astonishment. Feeling as if something were amiss he walked back to the Tutelary God's Temple, and by the time he had calmed down again he realized that his pile of dollars had gone. Since most of the people who ran gambling tables at the Festival were not natives of Weizhuang, where could he look for the culprits?

So white and glittering a pile of silver! All of it his . . . but now it had disappeared. Even to consider this tantamount to being robbed by his son did not comfort him. To consider himself as an insect did not comfort him either. This time he really tasted something of the bitterness of defeat.

But presently he changed defeat into victory. Raising his right hand he slapped his own face hard, twice, so that it tingled with pain. After this slapping his heart felt lighter, for it seemed as if the one who had given the slap was himself, the one slapped some other self, and soon it was just as if he had beaten someone else—in spite of the fact that his face was still tingling. He lay down satisfied that he had gained the victory.

Soon he was asleep.

CHAPTER 3

A Further Account of Ah Q's Victories

Although Ah Q was always gaining victories, it was only after he was favoured with a slap in the face by Mr. Zhao that he became famous.

After paying the bailiff two hundred cash he lay down angrily. Then he said to himself, 'What is the world coming to nowadays, with sons beating their fathers. . . .' And then the thought of the prestige of Mr. Zhao, who was now his son, gradually raised his spirits. He scrambled up and made his way to the tavern singing *The Young Widow at Her Husband's Grave*.[1] At that time he did feel that Mr. Zhao was a cut above most people.

After this incident, strange to relate, it was true that everybody seemed to pay him unusual respect. He probably attri-

---

[1] A local opera popular in Shaoxing.

buted this to the fact that he was Mr. Zhao's father, but actually such was not the case. In Weizhuang, as a rule, if the seventh child hit the eighth child or Li So-and-so hit Zhang So-and-so, it was not taken seriously. A beating had to be connected with some important personage like Mr. Zhao before the villagers thought it worth talking about. But once they thought it worth talking about, since the beater was famous the one beaten enjoyed some of his reflected fame. As for the fault being Ah Q's, that was naturally taken for granted, the reason being that Mr. Zhao could do no wrong. But if Ah Q were wrong, why did everybody seem to treat him with unusual respect? This is difficult to explain. We may put forward the hypothesis that it was because Ah Q had said he belonged to the same family as Mr. Zhao; thus, although he had been beaten, people were still afraid there might be some truth in his assertion and therefore thought it safer to treat him more respectfully. Or, alternatively, it may have been like the case of the sacrificial beef in the Confucian temple: although the beef was in the same category as the pork and mutton, being of animal origin just as they were, later Confucians did not dare touch it since the sage had enjoyed it.

After this Ah Q prospered for several years.

One spring, when he was walking along in a state of happy intoxication, he saw Whiskers Wang sitting stripped to the waist in the sunlight at the foot of a wall, catching lice; and at this sight his own body began to itch. Since Whiskers Wang was scabby and bewhiskered, everybody called him 'Ringworm Whiskers Wang'. Although Ah Q omitted the word 'Ringworm', he had the greatest contempt for the man. To Ah Q, while scabs were nothing to take exception to, such hairy cheeks were really too outlandish and could excite nothing but scorn. So Ah Q sat down by his side. Had it been any other idler, Ah Q would never have dared sit down so casually; but what had he to fear by the side of Whiskers Wang? In fact, his willingness to sit down was doing the fellow an honour.

Ah Q took off his tattered lined jacket and turned it inside out; but either because he had washed it recently or because he was too clumsy, a long search yielded only three or four lice. He saw that Whiskers Wang, on the other hand, was catching

first one and then another in swift succession, cracking them
between his teeth with a popping sound.

Ah Q felt first disappointed, then resentful: the despicable
Whiskers Wang had so many, he himself so few—what a great
loss of face! He longed to find one or two big ones, but there
were none, and when at last he managed to catch a middle-
sized one, stuffed it fiercely between his thick lips and bit hard,
the resultant pop was again inferior to the noise made by
Whiskers Wang.

All Ah Q's ringworm patches turned scarlet. He flung his
jacket on the ground, spat, and swore, 'Hairy worm!'

'Mangy dog, who are you calling names?' Whiskers Wang
looked up contemptuously.

Although the relative respect accorded him in recent years
had increased Ah Q's pride, he was still rather timid when
confronted by those loafers accustomed to fighting. But today
he was feeling exceptionally pugnacious. How dare a hairy-
cheeked creature like this insult him?

'If the cap fits wear it,' he retorted, standing up and putting
his hands on his hips.

'Are your bones itching?' demanded Whiskers Wang,
standing up too and draping his jacket over his shoulders.

Thinking that the fellow meant to run away, Ah Q lunged
forward to punch him. But before his fist reached the target, his
opponent seized him and gave him a tug which sent him
staggering. Then Whiskers Wang seized his queue and started
dragging him towards the wall to knock his head in the time-
honoured manner.

' "A gentleman uses his tongue but not his hands!" ' protested Ah Q, his head on one side.

Apparently Whiskers Wang was no gentleman, for without
paying the slightest attention to what Ah Q said he knocked
his head against the wall five times in succession, then with a
great push shoved him two yards away, after which he walked
off in triumph.

As far as Ah Q could remember, this was the first humiliation
of his life, because he had always scoffed at Whiskers Wang on
account of his ugly bewhiskered cheeks, but had never been
scoffed at, much less beaten by him. And now, contrary to all

expectations, Whiskers Wang had beaten him. Could it really be true, as they said in the market-place: 'The Emperor has abolished the official examinations, so that scholars who have passed them are no longer in demand'? This must have undermined the Zhao family's prestige. Was this why people were treating him contemptuously too?

Ah Q stood there irresolutely.

From the distance approached another of Ah Q's enemies. This was Mr. Qian's eldest son whom Ah Q thoroughly despised. After studying in a foreign-style school in the city, it seemed he had gone to Japan. When he came home half a year later his legs were straight[1] and his queue had disappeared. His mother wept bitterly a dozen times, and his wife tried three times to jump into the well. Later his mother told everyone, 'His queue was cut off by some scoundrel when he was drunk. By rights he ought to be a big official, but now he'll have to wait till it's grown again.' Ah Q, however, did not believe this, and insisted on calling him a 'Fake Foreign Devil' or 'Traitor in Foreign Pay'. At sight of him he would start cursing under his breath.

What Ah Q despised and detested most in him was his false queue. When it came to having a false queue, a man could scarcely be considered human; and the fact that his wife had not attempted to jump into the well a fourth time showed that she was not a good woman either.

Now this 'Fake Foreign Devil' was approaching.

'Baldhead! Ass . . .' In the past Ah Q had just cursed under his breath, inaudibly; but today, because he was in a rage and itching for revenge, the words slipped out involuntarily.

Unfortunately this Baldhead was carrying a shiny brown cane which looked to Ah Q like the 'staff carried by a mourner'. With great strides he bore down on Ah Q who, guessing at once that a beating was in the offing, hastily flexed his muscles and hunched his shoulders in anticipation. Sure enough, *Thwack!* something struck him on the head.

'I meant him!' explained Ah Q, pointing to a nearby child. *Thwack! Thwack! Thwack!*

[1] The stiff-legged stride of many foreigners led some Chinese to believe that their knees had no joints.

As far as Ah Q could remember, this was the second humiliation of his life. Fortunately after the thwacking stopped it seemed to him that the matter was closed, and he even felt somewhat relieved. Moreover, the precious 'ability to forget' handed down by his ancestors stood him in good stead. He walked slowly away and by the time he approached the tavern door he was quite cheerful again.

Just then, however, a small nun from the Convent of Quiet Self-Improvement came walking towards him. The sight of a nun always made Ah Q swear; how much more so, then, after these humiliations? When he recalled what had happened, his anger flared up again.

'I couldn't think what made my luck so bad today—so it's meeting you that did it!' he fumed to himself.

Going towards her he spat noisily. 'Ugh! . . . Pah!'

The small nun paid not the least attention but walked on with lowered head. Ah Q stepped up to her and shot out a hand to rub her newly shaved scalp, then with a guffaw cried, 'Baldhead! Go back quick, your monk's waiting for you. . . .'

'Who are you pawing? . . .' demanded the nun, flushing all over her face as she quickened her pace.

The men in the tavern roared with laughter. This appreciation of his feat added to Ah Q's elation.

'If the monk paws you, why can't I?' He pinched her cheek.

Again the men in the tavern roared with laughter. More bucked than ever, and eager to please his admirers, Ah Q pinched her hard again before letting her go.

This encounter had made him forget Whiskers Wang and the Fake Foreign Devil, as if all the day's bad luck had been avenged. And strange to relate, even more completely relaxed than after the thwacking, he felt as light as if he were walking on air.

'Ah Q, may you die sonless!' wailed the little nun already some distance away.

Ah Q roared with delighted laughter.

The men in the tavern joined in, with only a shade less gusto in their laughter.

CHAPTER 4
The Tragedy of Love

There are said to be some victors who take no pleasure in a victory unless their opponents are as fierce as tigers or eagles: in the case of foes as timid as sheep or chickens they find their triumph empty. There are other victors who, having carried all before them, with the enemy slain or surrendered, utterly cowed, realize that now no foe, no rival, no friend is left—none but themselves, supreme, lonely, lost, and forlorn. Then they find their triumph a tragedy. But not so our hero: he was always exultant. This may be a proof of the moral supremacy of China over the rest of the world.

Look at Ah Q, elated as if he were walking on air!

This victory was not without strange consequences, though. For after walking on air for quite a time he floated into the Tutelary God's Temple, where he would normally have started snoring as soon as he lay down. This evening, however, he found it very hard to close his eyes, being struck by something odd about his thumb and first finger, which seemed to be smoother than usual. It is impossible to say whether something soft and smooth on the little nun's face had stuck to his fingers, or whether his fingers had been rubbed smooth against her cheek.

'Ah Q, may you die sonless!'

These words sounded again in Ah Q's ears, and he thought, 'Quite right, I should take a wife; for if a man dies sonless he has no one to sacrifice a bowl of rice to his spirit . . . I ought to have a wife.' As the saying goes, 'There are three forms of unfilial conduct, of which the worst is to have no descendants',[1] and it is one of the tragedies of life that 'spirits without descendants go hungry'.[2] Thus his view was absolutely in accordance with the teachings of the saints and sages, and it is indeed a pity that later he should have run amok.

'Woman, woman! . . .' he thought.

[1] A quotation from Mencius (372–289 B.C.).
[2] A quotation from the old classic *Zuo Zhuan*.

'. . . The monk paws. . . . Woman, woman! . . . Woman!'
he thought again.

We shall never know when Ah Q finally fell asleep that
evening. After this, however, he probably always found his
fingers rather soft and smooth, and always remained a little
light-headed. 'Woman . . .' he kept thinking.

From this we can see that woman is a menace to mankind.

The majority of Chinese men could become saints and sages,
were it not for the unfortunate fact that they are ruined by
women. The Shang dynasty was destroyed by Da Ji, the Zhou
dynasty was undermined by Bao Si; as for the Qin dynasty,
although there is no historical evidence to that effect, if we
assume that it fell on account of some woman we shall probably
not be far wrong. And it is a fact that Dong Zhuo's death was
caused by Diao Chan.[1]

Ah Q, too, was a man of strict morals to begin with. Although
we do not know whether he was guided by some good teacher,
he had always shown himself most scrupulous in observing
'strict segregation of the sexes', and was righteous enough to
denounce such heretics as the little nun and the Fake Foreign
Devil. His view was, 'All nuns must carry on in secret with
monks. If a woman walks alone on the street, she must want to
seduce bad men. When a man and a woman talk together, it
must be to arrange to meet.' In order to correct such people,
he would glare furiously, pass loud, cutting remarks, or, if the
place were deserted, throw a small stone from behind.

Who could tell that close on thirty, when a man should 'stand
firm',[2] he would lose his head like this over a little nun? Such
light-headedness, according to the classical canons, is most
reprehensible; thus women certainly are hateful creatures.
For if the little nun's face had not been soft and smooth, Ah Q
would not have been bewitched by her; nor would this have
happened if the little nun's face had been covered by a cloth.
Five or six years before, when watching an open-air opera, he

---

[1] Da Ji, in the twelfth century B.C., was the concubine of the last king of the
Shang dynasty. Bao Si, in the eighth century B.C., was the concubine of the last
king of the Western Zhou dynasty. Diao Chan was the concubine of Dong Zhuo,
a powerful warlord at the end of the Han dynasty.

[2] Confucius said that at thirty he 'stood firm'. The phrase was later used to
indicate that a man was thirty years old.

had pinched the leg of a woman in the audience; but because it was separated from him by the cloth of her trousers he had not had this light-headed feeling afterwards. The little nun had not covered her face, however, and this is another proof of the odiousness of the heretic.

'Woman . . .' thought Ah Q.

He kept a close watch on those women who he believed must 'want to seduce men', but they did not smile at him. He listened very carefully to those women who talked to him, but not one of them mentioned anything relevant to a secret rendezvous. Ah! This was simply another example of the odiousness of women: they all assumed a false modesty.

One day when Ah Q was grinding rice in Mr. Zhao's house, he sat down in the kitchen after supper to smoke a pipe. If it had been anyone else's house, he could have gone home after supper, but they dined early in the Zhao family. Although it was the rule that you must not light a lamp but go to bed after eating, there were occasional exceptions to the rule. Before Mr. Zhao's son passed the county examination he was allowed to light a lamp to study the examination essays, and when Ah Q went to do odd jobs he was allowed to light a lamp to grind rice. Because of this latter exception to the rule, Ah Q still sat in the kitchen smoking before going on with his work.

When Amah Wu, the only maidservant in the Zhao household, had finished washing the dishes, she sat down on the long bench too and started chatting to Ah Q:

'Our mistress hasn't eaten anything for two days, because the master wants to get a concubine. . . .'

'Woman . . . Amah Wu . . . this little widow,' thought Ah Q.

'Our young mistress is going to have a baby in the eighth moon. . . .'

'Woman . . .' thought Ah Q.

He put down his pipe and stood up.

'Our young mistress—' Amah Wu chattered on.

'Sleep with me!' Ah Q suddenly rushed forward and threw himself at her feet.

There was a moment of absolute silence.

'Ai-ya!' Dumbfounded for an instant, Amah Wu suddenly

began to tremble, then rushed out shrieking and could soon be heard sobbing.

Ah Q kneeling opposite the wall was dumbfounded too. He grasped the empty bench with both hands and stood up slowly, dimly aware that something was wrong. In fact, by this time he was in rather a nervous state himself. In a flurry, he stuck his pipe into his belt and decided to go back to grind rice. But— *Bang!*—a heavy blow landed on his head, and he spun round to see the successful county candidate standing before him brandishing a big bamboo pole.

'How dare you . . . you . . .'

The big bamboo pole came down across Ah Q's shoulders. When he put up both hands to protect his head, the blow landed on his knuckles, causing him considerable pain. As he escaped through the kitchen door it seemed as if his back also received a blow.

'Turtle's egg!' shouted the successful candidate, cursing him in mandarin from behind.

Ah Q fled to the hulling-floor where he stood alone, his knuckles still aching and still remembering that 'Turtle's egg!' because it was an expression never used by the Weizhuang villagers but only by the rich who had seen something of official life. This made it the more alarming, the more impressive. By now, however, all thought of 'Woman . . .' had flown. After this cursing and beating it seemed as if something were done with, and quite light-heartedly he began to grind rice again. Soon this made him hot, and he stopped to take off his shirt.

While taking off his shirt he heard an uproar outside, and since Ah Q was all for excitement he went out in search of the sound. Step by step he traced it into Mr. Zhao's inner courtyard. Although it was dusk he could see many people there: all the Zhao family including the mistress who had not eaten for two days. In addition, their neighbour Mrs. Zou was there, as well as their relatives Zhao Baiyen and Zhao Sichen.

The young mistress was leading Amah Wu out of the servants' quarters, saying as she did so:

'Come outside . . . don't stay brooding in your own room.'

'Everybody knows you are a good woman,' put in Mrs. Zou from the side. 'You mustn't think of committing suicide.'

Amah Wu merely wailed, muttering something inaudible.

'This is interesting,' thought Ah Q. 'What mischief can this little widow be up to?' Wanting to find out, he was approaching Zhao Sichen when suddenly he caught sight of Mr. Zhao's eldest son rushing towards him with, what was worse, the big bamboo pole in his hand. The sight of this big bamboo pole reminded him that he had been beaten by it, and he realized that apparently he was connected in some way with all this excitement. He turned and ran, hoping to escape to the hulling-floor, not foreseeing that the bamboo pole would cut off his retreat. When it did, he turned and ran in the other direction, leaving without further ado by the back gate. Soon he was back in the Tutelary God's Temple.

After Ah Q had been sitting down for a time, he broke out in goose-flesh and felt cold, because although it was spring the nights were still chilly and not suited to bare backs. He remembered that he had left his shirt in the Zhaos' house but was afraid that if he went to fetch it he might get another taste of the successful candidate's bamboo pole.

Then the bailiff came in.

'Curse you, Ah Q!' said the bailiff. 'So you can't even keep your hands off the Zhao family servants, you rebel! You've made me lose my sleep, damn it! . . .'

Under this torrent of abuse Ah Q naturally had nothing to say. Finally, since it was night-time, he had to pay the bailiff double: four hundred cash. Because he happened to have no ready money by him, he gave his felt hat as security, and agreed to the following five terms:

1. The next morning Ah Q must take a pair of red candles, weighing one pound each, and a bundle of incense sticks to the Zhao family to atone for his misdeeds.

2. Ah Q must pay for the Taoist priests whom the Zhao family had called to exorcize evil spirits.

3. Ah Q must never again set foot in the Zhao household.

4. If anything unfortunate should happen to Amah Wu, Ah Q must be held responsible.

5. Ah Q must not go back for his wages or shirt.

Ah Q naturally agreed to everything, but unfortunately he had no ready money. Luckily it was already spring, so it was possible to do without his padded quilt which he pawned for two thousand cash to comply with the terms stipulated. After kowtowing with bare back he still had a few cash left, but instead of using these to redeem his felt hat from the bailiff, he spent them all on drink.

Actually, the Zhao family burned neither the incense nor the candles, because these could be used when the mistress worshipped Buddha and were put aside for that purpose. Most of the ragged shirt was made into diapers for the baby which was born to the young mistress in the eighth moon, while the tattered remainder was used by Amah Wu to make shoe-soles.

CHAPTER 5

The Problem of Making a Living

After Ah Q had kowtowed and complied with the Zhao family's terms, he went back as usual to the Tutelary God's Temple. The sun had gone down, and he began to feel that something was wrong. Careful thought led him to the conclusion that this was probably because his back was bare. Remembering that he still had a ragged lined jacket, he put it on and lay down, and when he opened his eyes again the sun was already shining on the top of the west wall. He sat up, saying, 'Curse it. . . .'

After getting up he loafed about the streets as usual, until he began to feel that something else was wrong, though this was not to be compared to the physical discomfort of a bare back. Apparently, from that day onwards all the women in Weizhuang fought shy of Ah Q: whenever they saw him coming they took refuge indoors. In fact, even Mrs. Zou who was nearing fifty retreated in confusion with the rest, calling her eleven-year-old daughter to go inside. This struck Ah Q as very strange. 'The bitches!' he thought. 'All of a sudden they're behaving like young ladies. . . .'

A good many days later, however, he felt even more forcibly

that something was wrong. First, the tavern refused him credit; secondly, the old man in charge of the Tutelary God's Temple made some uncalled-for remarks, as if he wanted Ah Q to leave; and thirdly, for many days—how many exactly he could not remember—not a soul had come to hire him. To be refused credit in the tavern he could put up with; if the old man kept urging him to leave, he could just ignore his complaints; but when no one came to hire him he had to go hungry, and this was really a 'cursed' state to be in.

When Ah Q could stand it no longer he went to his former employers' homes to find out what was the matter—it was only Mr. Zhao's threshold that he was not allowed to cross. But he met with a strange reception. The one to appear was always a man looking thoroughly annoyed who waved him away as if he were a beggar, saying:

'There's nothing for you, get out!'

Ah Q found it more and more extraordinary. 'These people always needed help in the past,' he thought. 'They can't suddenly have nothing to be done. This looks fishy.' After making careful inquiries he found out that when they had any odd jobs they all called in Young D. Now this Young D was a thin and weakly pauper, even lower in Ah Q's eyes than Whiskers Wang. Who could have thought that this low fellow would steal his living from him? So this time Ah Q's indignation was greater than usual, and going on his way, fuming, he suddenly raised his arm and sang: 'Steel mace in hand I shall trounce you. . . .'[1]

A few days later he did indeed meet Young D in front of Mr. Qian's house. 'When two foes meet, there is no mistaking each other.' As Ah Q advanced upon him, Young D stood his ground.

'Beast!' spluttered Ah Q, glaring.

'I'm an insect—will that do? . . .' rejoined Young D.

Such modesty only enraged Ah Q even more, but since he had no steel mace in his hand all he could do was rush forward to grab at Young D's queue. Young D, protecting his own queue with one hand, grabbed at Ah Q's with the other, whereupon Ah Q also used his free hand to protect his own queue. In the past Ah Q had never considered Young D worth taking

[1] A line from *The Battle of the Dragon and the Tiger*, an opera popular in Shaoxing.

seriously, but owing to his recent privations he was now as thin and weak as his opponent, so that they presented a spectacle of evenly matched antagonists, four hands clutching at two heads, both men bending at the waist, casting a blue, rainbow-shaped shadow on the Qian family's white wall for over half an hour.

'All right! All right!' exclaimed some of the onlookers, probably by way of mediation.

'Good, good!' exclaimed others, but whether to mediate, applaud the fighters, or spur them on to further efforts, is not certain.

The two combatants turned deaf ears to them all, however. If Ah Q advanced three paces, Young D would recoil three paces, and there they would stand. If Young D advanced three paces, Ah Q would recoil three paces, and there they would stand again. After about half an hour—Weizhuang had few clocks, so it is difficult to tell the time; it may have been twenty minutes—when steam was rising from their heads and sweat pouring down their cheeks, Ah Q let fall his hands, and in the same second Young D's hands fell too. They straightened up simultaneously and stepped back simultaneously, pushing their way out through the crowd.

'Just you wait, curse you! . . .' called Ah Q over his shoulder.

'Curse you! Just you wait . . .' echoed Young D, also over his shoulder.

This epic struggle had apparently ended in neither victory nor defeat, and it is not known whether the spectators were satisfied or not, for none of them expressed any opinion. But still not a soul came to hire Ah Q for odd jobs.

One warm day, when a balmy breeze seemed to give some foretaste of summer, Ah Q actually felt cold; but he could put up with this—his greatest worry was an empty stomach. His cotton quilt, felt hat, and shirt had long since disappeared, and after that he had sold his padded jacket. Now nothing was left but his trousers, and these of course he could not take off. He had a ragged lined jacket, it is true; but this was certainly worthless, unless he gave it away to be made into shoe-soles. He had long been dreaming of finding some money on the road, but hitherto he had not come across any; he had also been hoping he might suddenly discover some money in his tumble-down room, and had frantically ransacked it, but the room was quite, quite empty. Then he made up his mind to go out in search of food.

As he walked along the road 'in search of food' he saw the familiar tavern and the familiar steamed bread, but he passed them by without pausing for a second, without even hankering after them. It was not these he was looking for, although what exactly he was looking for he did not know himself.

Since Weizhuang was not a big place, he soon left it behind. Most of the country outside the village consisted of paddy fields, green as far as the eye could see with the tender shoots of young rice, dotted here and there with round black, moving objects—peasants cultivating their fields. But blind to the delights of country life, Ah Q simply went on his way, for he knew instinctively that this was far removed from his 'search for food'. Finally, however, he came to the walls of the Convent of Quiet Self-Improvement.

The convent too was surrounded by paddy fields, its white walls standing out sharply in the fresh green, and inside the low earthen wall at the back was a vegetable garden. Ah Q hesitated for a time, looking around him. Since there was no one in sight he scrambled on to the low wall, holding on to some milkwort. The mud wall started crumbling, and Ah Q shook with fear; however, by clutching at the branch of a mulberry tree he managed to jump over it. Within was a wild profusion of vegetation, but no sign of yellow wine, steamed bread, or anything edible. A clump of bamboos by the west wall had put forth many young shoots, but unfortunately these were not cooked. There was also rape which had long since gone to seed, mustard already about to flower, and some tough old cabbages.

Resentful as a scholar who has failed the examinations, Ah Q walked slowly towards the gate of the garden. Suddenly, however, he gave a start of joy, for what did he see there but a patch of turnips! He knelt down and had just begun pulling when a round head appeared from behind the gate, only to be promptly withdrawn. This was no other than the little nun. Now though Ah Q had always had the greatest contempt for such people as little nuns, there are times when 'Discretion is the better part of valour'. He hastily pulled up four turnips, tore off the leaves, and stuffed them under his jacket. By this time an old nun had already come out.

'May Buddha preserve us, Ah Q! How dare you climb into our garden to steal turnips! . . . Mercy on us, what a wicked thing to do! Ai-ya, Buddha preserve us! . . .'

'When did I ever climb into your garden and steal turnips?' retorted Ah Q as he started off, keeping his eyes on her.

'Now—aren't you?' The old nun pointed at the bulge in his jacket.

'Are these yours? Will they come when you call? You . . . '

Leaving his sentence unfinished, Ah Q took to his heels as fast as he could, followed by a huge fat black dog. Originally this dog had been at the front gate, and how it reached the back garden was a mystery. With a snarl the black dog gave chase and was just about to bite Ah Q's leg when most opportunely a turnip fell from his jacket, and the dog, taken by surprise, stopped for a second. During this time Ah Q scrambled up the mulberry tree, scaled the mud wall, and fell, turnips and all, outside the convent. He left the black dog still barking by the mulberry tree, and the old nun saying her prayers.

Fearing that the nun would let the black dog out again, Ah Q gathered together his turnips and ran, picking up a few small stones as he went. But the black dog did not reappear. Ah Q threw away the stones and walked on, eating as he went, thinking to himself: 'There is nothing to be had here: better go to town. . . .'

By the time the third turnip was finished he had made up his mind to go to town.

CHAPTER 6
From Resurgence to Decline

Weizhuang did not see Ah Q again till just after the Moon
Festival that year. Everybody was surprised to hear of his
return, and this made them think back and wonder where he
had been all that time. In the past Ah Q had usually taken
great pleasure in announcing his few visits to town; but since
he had not done so this time, his going had passed unnoticed.
He may have told the old man in charge of the Tutelary God's
Temple, but according to the custom of Weizhuang only a trip
to town by Mr. Zhao, Mr. Qian, or the successful county
candidate counted as important. Even the Fake Foreign
Devil's going was not talked about, much less Ah Q's. This
would explain why the old man had not spread the news for
him, with the result that the villagers remained in the dark.

Ah Q's return this time was very different from before, and in
fact quite enough to occasion astonishment. The day was
growing dark when he showed up, bleary-eyed, at the tavern
door, walked up to the counter, and tossed down on it a handful
of silver and coppers produced from his belt. 'Cash!' he
announced. 'Bring the wine!' He was wearing a new lined
jacket and at his waist hung a large purse, the great weight of
which caused his belt to sag in a sharp curve.

It was the custom in Weizhuang that anyone in any way
unusual should be treated with respect rather than disregarded,
and now, although they knew quite well that this was Ah Q,
still he was very different from the Ah Q of the ragged coat.
The ancients say, 'A scholar who has been away three days
must be looked at with new eyes.' So the waiter, tavern-keeper,
customers, and passers-by all quite naturally expressed a kind
of suspicion mingled with respect. The tavern-keeper started
off by nodding, following this up with the words:

'So you're back, Ah Q!'

'Yes, I'm back.'

'Made a pretty packet, eh? . . . Where . . .?'

'I've been in town.'

By the next day this piece of news had spread through Weizhuang. And since everybody wanted to hear the success story of this Ah Q of the ready money and the new lined jacket, in the tavern, tea-house, and under the temple eaves, the villagers gradually ferreted out the news. The result was that they began to treat Ah Q with a new deference.

According to Ah Q, he had been a servant in the house of a successful provincial candidate. This part of the story filled all who heard it with awe. This successful provincial candidate was named Bai, but because he was the only successful provincial candidate in the whole town there was no need to use his surname: whenever anyone spoke of the successful provincial candidate, it meant him. And this was so not only in Weizhuang, for almost everyone within a radius of thirty miles imagined his name to be Mr. Successful Provincial Candidate. To have worked in the household of such a man naturally called for respect; but according to Ah Q's further statements, he was unwilling to go on working there because this successful candidate was really too much of a 'turtle's egg'. This part of the story made all who heard it sigh, but with a sense of pleasure, because it showed that Ah Q was unworthy to work in the household of such a man, yet not to work there was a pity.

According to Ah Q, his return was also due to his dissatisfaction with the townspeople because they called a long bench a straight bench, used shredded shallots to fry fish, and—a defect he had recently discovered—the women did not sway in a very satisfactory manner as they walked. However, the town had its good points too; for instance, in Weizhuang everyone played with thirty-two bamboo counters and only the Fake Foreign Devil could play mah-jong, but in town even the street urchins excelled at mah-jong. You had only to place the Fake Foreign Devil in the hands of these young rascals in their teens for him straightway to become like 'a small devil before the King of Hell'. This part of the story made all who heard it blush.

'Have you seen an execution?' asked Ah Q. 'Ah, that's a fine sight. . . . When they execute the revolutionaries. . . . Ah, that's a fine sight, a fine sight. . . .' He shook his head, sending his spittle flying on to the face of Zhao Sichen who was standing opposite him. This part of the story made all who heard it tremble. Then with a glance around, he suddenly raised his right hand and dropped it on the neck of Whiskers Wang who, craning forward, was listening with rapt attention.

'Off with his head!' shouted Ah Q.

Whiskers Wang gave a start, and jerked back his head as fast as lightning or a spark struck from a flint, while the bystanders shivered with pleasurable apprehension. After this, Whiskers Wang went about in a daze for many days and dared not go near Ah Q, nor did the others.

Although we cannot say that in the eyes of the inhabitants of Weizhuang Ah Q's status at this time was superior to that of Mr. Zhao, we can at least affirm without any danger of inaccuracy that it was approximately equivalent.

Not long after, Ah Q's fame suddenly spread into the women's apartments of Weizhuang too. Although the only two families of any pretensions in Weizhuang were those of Qian and Zhao, and nine-tenths of the rest were poor, still women's apartments are women's apartments, and the way Ah Q's fame spread into them was quite miraculous. When the womenfolk met they would say to each other, 'Mrs. Zou bought a blue silk skirt from Ah Q. Although it was old, it only cost ninety cents. And Zhao Baiyen's mother (this has yet to be verified, because some say it was Zhao Sichen's mother) bought a child's costume of crimson foreign calico which was nearly new for only three hundred cash, less eight per cent discount.'

Then those who had no silk skirt or needed foreign calico were most anxious to see Ah Q in order to buy from him. Far from avoiding him now, they sometimes followed him when he passed, calling to him to stop.

'Ah Q, have you any more silk skirts?' they would ask. 'No? We want foreign calico too. Do you have any?'

This news later spread from the poor households to the rich ones, because Mrs. Zou was so pleased with her silk skirt that she took it to Mrs. Zhao for her approval, and Mrs. Zhao told Mr. Zhao, speaking very highly of it.

Mr. Zhao discussed the matter that evening at dinner with his son the successful county candidate, suggesting that there was certainly something strange about Ah Q and that they should be more careful about their doors and windows. They did not know, though, what if anything Ah Q had left—he might still have something good. Since Mrs. Zhao happened to want a good cheap fur jacket, after a family council it was decided to ask Mrs. Zou to find Ah Q for them at once. For this a third exception was made to the rule, special permission being given that evening for a lamp to be lit.

A considerable amount of oil had been burned, but still there was no sign of Ah Q. The whole Zhao household was yawning with impatience, some of them resenting Ah Q's casualness, others blaming Mrs. Zou for not making a greater effort. Mrs. Zhao was afraid that Ah Q dared not come because of the terms agreed upon that spring, but Mr. Zhao did not think this anything to worry about because, as he said, 'This time *I* sent for him.' Sure enough, Mr. Zhao proved himself a man of insight, for Ah Q finally arrived with Mrs. Zou.

'He keeps saying he has nothing left,' panted Mrs. Zou as she came in. 'When I told him to come and tell you so himself he kept talking back. I told him . . .'

'Sir!' cried Ah Q with an attempt at a smile, coming to a halt under the eaves.

'I hear you did well for yourself in town, Ah Q,' said Mr. Zhao, going up to him and looking him over carefully. 'Very good. Now . . . they say you have some old things. . . . Bring them all here for us to look at. This is simply because I happen to want . . .'

'I told Mrs. Zou—there's nothing left.'

'Nothing left?' Mrs. Zhao could not help sounding disappointed. 'How could they go so quickly?'

'They belonged to a friend, and there wasn't much to begin with. People bought some. . . .'

'There must be something left.'

'Only a door curtain.'

'Then bring the door curtain for us to see,' said Mrs. Zhao hurriedly.

'Well, tomorrow will do,' said Mr. Zhao without much enthusiasm. 'When you have anything in future, Ah Q, you must bring it to us first. . . .'

'We certainly won't pay less than other people!' said the successful county candidate. His wife shot a hasty glance at Ah Q to see his reaction.

'I need a fur jacket,' said Mrs. Zhao.

Although Ah Q agreed, he slouched out so carelessly that they did not know whether he had taken their instructions to heart or not. This so disappointed, annoyed, and worried Mr. Zhao that he even stopped yawning. The successful candidate was also far from satisfied with Ah Q's attitude. 'People should be on their guard against such a turtle's egg,' he said. 'It might be best to order the bailiff to forbid him to live in Weizhuang.'

Mr. Zhao did not agree, saying that then Ah Q might bear a grudge, and that in a business like this it was probably a case of 'the eagle does not prey on its own nest': his own village need not worry so long as they were a little more watchful at night. The successful candidate, much impressed by this parental instruction, immediately withdrew his proposal for banishing Ah Q but cautioned Mrs. Zou on no account to repeat what had been said.

The next day, however, when Mrs. Zou took her blue skirt to be dyed black she repeated these insinuations about Ah Q, although not actually mentioning what the successful candidate had said about driving him away. Even so, it was most damaging to Ah Q. In the first place, the bailiff appeared at his door and took away the door curtain. Although Ah Q protested that Mrs. Zhao wanted to see it, the bailiff would not give it back and even demanded monthly hush money. In the second place, the villagers' respect for Ah Q suddenly changed. Although they still dared not take liberties, they avoided him as much as possible. While this differed from their previous fear of his 'Off with his head!' it closely resembled the attitude of the ancients to spirits: they kept a respectful distance.

Some idlers who wanted to get to the bottom of the business went to question Ah Q carefully. And with no attempt at concealment Ah Q told them proudly of his experiences. They learned that he had merely been a petty thief, not only unable to climb walls but even unable to go through openings: he simply stood outside an opening to receive the stolen goods.

One night he had just received a package and his chief had gone in again, when he heard a great uproar inside and took to his heels as fast as he could. He fled from the town that same night, back to Weizhuang; and after this he dared not return to do any more thieving. This story, however, was even more damaging to Ah Q, since the villagers had been keeping a respectful distance because they did not want to incur his enmity; for who could have guessed that he was only a thief who dared not steal again? Now they knew he was really too low to inspire fear.

CHAPTER 7

The Revolution

On the fourteenth day of the ninth moon of the third year in the reign of Emperor Xuan Tong[1]—the day on which Ah Q sold his purse to Zhao Baiyen—at midnight, after the fourth stroke of the third watch, a large boat with a big black awning arrived at the Zhao family's landing-place. This boat floated up in the darkness while the villagers were sound asleep, so that they knew nothing about it; but it left again about dawn, when quite a number of people saw it. Investigation revealed that this boat actually belonged to the successful provincial candidate!

This incident caused great uneasiness in Weizhuang, and before midday the hearts of all the villagers were beating faster. The Zhao family kept very quiet about the errand of the boat, but according to gossip in the tea-house and tavern, the revolutionaries were going to enter the town and the successful provincial candidate had come to the country to take refuge. Mrs. Zou alone thought otherwise, maintaining that the successful candidate merely wanted to deposit a few battered cases in Weizhuang, but that Mr. Zhao had sent them back. Actually the successful provincial candidate and the successful county candidate in the Zhao family were not on good terms, so that it was scarcely logical to expect them to prove friends in adversity; moreover, since Mrs. Zou was a neighbour of the Zhao

[1] 4 November 1911, the day on which Shaoxing was freed in the 1911 Revolution.

family and had a better idea of what was going on, she ought to have known.

Then a rumour spread to the effect that although the scholar had not come in person, he had sent a long letter tracing some distant relationship with the Zhao family; and since Mr. Zhao after thinking it over had decided it could after all do him no harm to keep the cases, they were now stowed under his wife's bed. As for the revolutionaries, some people said they had entered the town that night in white helmets and white armour—in mourning for Emperor Chong Zheng.[1]

Ah Q had long since known of revolutionaries and this year with his own eyes had seen revolutionaries decapitated. But since it had occurred to him that the revolutionaries were rebels and that a rebellion would make things difficult for him, he had always detested and kept away from them. Who could have guessed that they could strike such fear into a successful provincial candidate renowned for thirty miles around? In consequence, Ah Q could not help feeling rather fascinated, the terror of all the villagers only adding to his delight.

'Revolution is not a bad thing,' thought Ah Q. 'Finish off the whole lot of them . . . curse them! . . . I'd like to go over to the revolutionaries myself.'

Ah Q had been hard up recently, which no doubt made him rather dissatisfied; moreover he had drunk two bowls of wine at noon on an empty stomach. Consequently he became drunk very quickly; and as he walked along thinking to himself, he seemed again to be treading on air. Suddenly, in some curious way, he felt as if he were a revolutionary and all the people in Weizhuang were his captives. Unable to contain himself for joy, he shouted at the top of his voice:

'Rebellion! Rebellion!'

All the villagers stared at him in consternation. Ah Q had never seen such pitiful looks before; they refreshed him as much as a drink of iced water in summer. So he walked on even more happily, shouting:

'Fine! . . . I shall take what I want! I shall like whom I please!

[1] Chong Zheng, the last emperor of the Ming dynasty, reigned from 1628 to 1644. He hanged himself before the Manchus entered Peking.

'De-de, qiang-qiang!
Alas, in my cups I have slain my sworn brother Zheng.
Alas, ya-ya-ya . . .
De-de, qiang-qiang, de, qiang-ling-qiang!
Steel mace in hand I shall trounce you.'

Mr. Zhao and his son were standing at their gate with two relatives discussing the revolution. Ah Q did not see them as he passed with his head thrown back, singing, 'De-de . . .'

'Q, old fellow!' called Mr. Zhao timidly in a low voice.

'De-de,' sang Ah Q, unable to imagine that his name could be linked with those words 'old fellow'. Sure that he had heard wrongly and was in no way concerned, he simply went on singing, 'De, qiang, qiang-ling-qiang, qiang!'

'Q, old fellow!'

'Alas, in my cups . . .'

'Ah Q!' The successful candidate had no choice but to name him outright.

Only then did Ah Q come to a stop. 'Well?' he asked with his head on one side.

'Q, old fellow, . . . now . . .' But Mr. Zhao was at a loss for words again. 'Are you well off now?'

'Well off? Of course. I get what I want. . . .'

'Ah Q, old man, poor friends of yours like us are of no consequence. . . .' faltered Zhao Baiyen, as if sounding out the revolutionaries' attitude.

'Poor friends? You're richer anyway than I am.' With this Ah Q walked away.

This left them in speechless dismay. Back home that evening Mr. Zhao and his son discussed the question until it was time to light the lamps. And Zhao Baiyen once home took the purse from his waist and gave it to his wife to hide for him at the bottom of a chest.

For a while Ah Q walked upon air, but by the time he reached the Tutelary God's Temple he had come down to earth again. That evening the old man in charge of the temple was also unexpectedly friendly and offered him tea. Then Ah Q asked him for two flat cakes, and after eating these demanded a four-ounce candle that had been lighted once and a candlestick. He lit the candle and lay down alone in his little room feeling inexpressibly refreshed and happy, while the candlelight leaped and flickered as if this were the Lantern Festival and his imagination soared with it.

'Revolt? It would be fine. . . . A troop of revolutionaries would come, all in white helmets and white armour, with swords, steel maces, bombs, foreign guns, sharp-pointed double-edged knives, and spears with hooks. When they passed this temple they would call out, "Ah Q! Come along with us!" And then I would go with them. . . .

'Then the fun would start. All the villagers, the whole lousy lot, would kneel down and plead, "Ah Q, spare us!" But who would listen to them! The first to die would be Young D and Mr. Zhao, then the successful county candidate and the Fake Foreign Devil. . . . But perhaps I would spare a few. I would once have spared Whiskers Wang, but now I don't even want him. . . .

'Things . . . I would go straight in and open the cases: silver ingots, foreign coins, foreign calico jackets. . . . First I would move the Ningpo bed of the successful county candidate's wife to the temple, as well as the Qian family tables and chairs—or else just use the Zhao family's. I wouldn't lift a finger myself, but order Young D to move the things for me, and to look smart about it if he didn't want his face slapped. . . .

'Zhao Sichen's younger sister is very ugly. In a few years Mrs. Zou's daughter might be worth considering. The Fake Foreign Devil's wife is willing to sleep with a man without a queue, hah! She can't be a good woman! The successful county candidate's wife has scars on her eyelids. . . . I haven't seen Amah Wu for a long time and don't know where she is—what a pity her feet are so big.'

Before Ah Q had reached a satisfactory conclusion, there was a sound of snoring. The four-ounce candle had burned down only half an inch, and its flickering red light lit up his open mouth.

'Ho, ho!' shouted Ah Q suddenly, raising his head and looking wildly around. But at sight of the four-ounce candle, he lay back and fell asleep again.

The next morning he got up very late, and when he went out into the street everything was the same as usual. He was still hungry, but though he racked his brains he did not seem able to think of anything. All of a sudden, however, an idea struck him and he walked slowly off until, either by design or accident, he reached the Convent of Quiet Self-Improvement.

The convent was as peaceful as it had been that spring, with its white wall and shining black gate. After a moment's reflection he knocked at the gate, whereupon a dog on the other side started barking. He hastily picked up some broken bricks, then went back again to knock more heavily, knocking until the black gate was pitted with pock-marks. At last he heard someone coming to open up.

Clutching a brick, Ah Q straddled there prepared to do battle with the black dog. The convent gate opened a crack, but no black dog rushed out. When he looked in all he could see was the old nun.

'What are you here for again?' she asked with a start.

'There's a revolution . . . didn't you know?' said Ah Q vaguely.

'Revolution, revolution . . . we've already had one.' The old nun's eyes were red. 'What more do you want to do to us?'

'What?' demanded Ah Q, dumbfounded.

'Didn't you know? The revolutionaries have already been here!'

'Who?' demanded Ah Q, still more dumbfounded.

'The successful county candidate and the Foreign Devil.'

This completely took the wind out of Ah Q's sails. When the old nun saw there was no fight left in him she promptly shut the gate, so that when Ah Q pushed it again he could not budge it, and when he knocked again there was no answer.

It had happened that morning. The successful county candidate in the Zhao family was quick to learn the news. As soon as he heard that the revolutionaries had entered the town that night, he wound his queue up on his head and went out first thing to call on the Fake Foreign Devil in the Qian family, with whom he had never been on very good terms. Because this was a time for all to work for reforms, they had a most satisfactory talk and on the spot became comrades who saw eye to eye and pledged themselves to make revolution.

After racking their brains for some time, they remembered

that in the Convent of Quiet Self-Improvement there was an imperial tablet inscribed 'Long live the Emperor' which ought to be done away with immediately. Thereupon they lost no time in going to the convent to carry out their revolutionary activities. Because the old nun tried to stop them and passed a few remarks, they considered her as the Manchu government and gave her quite a few knocks on the head with a stick and with their knuckles. The nun, pulling herself together after they had gone, made an inspection. Naturally the imperial tablet had been smashed into fragments on the ground and the valuable Xuan De censer[1] before the shrine of Guanyin, the goddess of mercy, had also disappeared.

Ah Q only learned this later. He deeply regretted having been asleep at the time, and resented the fact that they had not come to call him. Then he said to himself, 'Maybe they still don't know I have joined the revolutionaries.'

CHAPTER 8

Barred from the Revolution

The people of Weizhuang felt easier in their minds with each passing day. From the news brought they knew that although the revolutionaries had entered the town their coming had not made a great deal of difference. The magistrate was still the highest official, it was only his title that had changed; and the successful provincial candidate also had some post—the Weizhuang villagers could not remember these names clearly—some kind of official post; while the head of the military was still the same old captain. The only cause for alarm was that, the day after their arrival, some bad revolutionaries made trouble by cutting off people's queues. It was said that the boatman Seven Pounder from the next village had fallen into their clutches, and that he no longer looked presentable. Still, the danger of this was not great, because the Weizhuang villagers seldom went to town to begin with, and those who had been considering

[1] Highly decorative bronze censers were made during the Xuan De period (1426–35) of the Ming dynasty.

a trip there at once changed their minds in order to avoid this risk. Ah Q had been thinking of going to town to look up his old friends, but as soon as he heard the news he gave up the idea.

It would be wrong, however, to say that there were no reforms in Weizhuang. During the next few days the number of people who coiled their queues on their heads gradually increased and, as has already been said, the first to do so was naturally the successful county candidate; the next were Zhao Sichen and Zhao Baiyen, and after them Ah Q. If it had been summer it would not have been considered strange if everybody had coiled their queues on their heads or tied them in knots; but this was late autumn, so that this autumn observance of a summer practice on the part of those who coiled their queues could be considered nothing short of a heroic decision, and as far as Weizhuang was concerned it could not be said to have had no connection with the reforms.

When Zhao Sichen approached with the nape of his neck bare, people who saw him remarked, 'Ah! Here comes a revolutionary!'

When Ah Q heard this he was greatly impressed. Although he had long since heard how the successful county candidate had coiled his queue on his head, it had never occurred to him to do the same. Only now when he saw that Zhao Sichen had followed suit was he struck with the idea of doing the same himself. He made up his mind to copy them. He used a bamboo chopstick to twist his queue up on his head, and after some hesitation eventually summoned up the courage to go out.

As he walked along the street people looked at him, but without any comment. Ah Q, disgruntled at first, soon waxed indignant. Recently he had been losing his temper very easily. As a matter of fact he was no worse off than before the revolution, people treated him politely, and the shops no longer demanded payment in cash, yet Ah Q still felt dissatisfied. A revolution, he thought, should mean more than this. When he saw Young D, his anger boiled over.

Young D had also coiled his queue up on his head and, what was more, had actually used a bamboo chopstick to do so too. Ah Q had never imagined that Young D would also have the courage to do this; he certainly could not tolerate such a thing! Who was Young D anyway? He was greatly tempted to seize him then and there, break his bamboo chopstick, let down his queue and slap his face several times into the bargain to punish him for forgetting his place and for his presumption in becoming a revolutionary. But in the end he let him off, simply fixing him with a furious glare, spitting, and exclaiming, 'Pah!'

These last few days the only one to go to town was the Fake Foreign Devil. The successful county candidate in the Zhao family had thought of using the deposited cases as a pretext to call on the successful provincial candidate, but the danger that he might have his queue cut off had made him defer his visit. He had written an extremely formal letter, and asked the Fake Foreign Devil to take it to town; he had also asked the latter to introduce him to the Freedom Party. When the Fake Foreign Devil came back he collected four dollars from the successful county candidate, after which the latter wore a silver peach on his chest. All the Weizhuang villagers were overawed, and said that this was the badge of the Persimmon Oil Party,[1] equivalent to the rank of a Han Lin.[2] As a result, Mr. Zhao's prestige suddenly increased, far more so in fact than when his son first passed the official examination; consequently he started looking down on everyone else and when he saw Ah Q tended to ignore him a little.

Ah Q, disgruntled at finding himself cold-shouldered all the time, realized as soon as he heard of this silver peach why he was left out in the cold. Simply to say that you had gone over was not enough to make anyone a revolutionary; nor was it enough merely to wind your queue up on your head; the most important thing was to get into touch with the revolutionary party. In all his life he had known only two revolutionaries, one of whom had already lost his head in town, leaving only the Fake Foreign Devil. His only course was to go at once to talk things over with the Fake Foreign Devil.

The front gate of the Qian house happened to be open, and Ah Q crept timidly in. Once inside he gave a start, for there was

[1] The Freedom Party was called Zi You Dang. The villagers, not understanding the word 'freedom', turned Zi You into Shi You, which means persimmon oil.
[2] Member of the Imperial Academy in the Qing dynasty.

the Fake Foreign Devil standing in the middle of the courtyard
dressed entirely in black, no doubt in foreign dress, and also
wearing a silver peach. In his hand he held the stick with which
Ah Q was already acquainted to his cost, while the foot-long
queue which he had grown again had been combed out to
hang loosely over his shoulders, giving him a resemblance to
the immortal Liu Hai.[1] Standing respectfully before him were
Zhao Baiyen and three others, all of them listening with the
utmost deference to what the Fake Foreign Devil was saying.

Ah Q tiptoed inside and stood behind Zhao Baiyen, eager to
pronounce some greeting, but not knowing what to say.
Obviously he could not call the man 'Fake Foreign Devil',
and neither 'Foreigner' nor 'Revolutionary' seemed quite the
thing. Perhaps the best form of address would be 'Mr.
Foreigner'.

But Mr. Foreigner had not seen him, because with eyes
upraised he was holding forth with great gusto:

'I am so impetuous that when we met I kept urging, "Old
Hong, let's get down to business!" But he always answered
"*Nein!*"—that's a foreign word which you wouldn't understand.
Otherwise we should have succeeded long ago. This just goes
to show how cautious he is. Time and again he asked me to go
to Hupeh, but I've not yet agreed. Who wants to work in a
small district town? . . .'

'Er—well—' Ah Q waited for him to pause, then screwed up
his courage to speak. But for some reason or other he still did
not call him Mr. Foreigner.

The four men who had been listening gave a start and
turned to stare at Ah Q. Mr. Foreigner too caught sight of him
for the first time.

'What is it?'

'I . . .'

'Clear out!'

'I want to join . . .'

'Get out!' Mr. Foreigner raised the 'mourner's stick'.

Thereupon Zhao Baiyen and the others shouted, 'Mr. Qian
tells you to get out, don't you hear!'

Ah Q put up his hands to protect his head, and without

[1] A figure in Chinese folk legend, portrayed with flowing hair.

knowing what he was doing fled through the gate; but this
time Mr. Foreigner did not give chase. After running more
than sixty steps Ah Q slowed down, and now his heart filled
with dismay, because if Mr. Foreigner would not allow him to
be a revolutionary, there was no other way open to him. In
future he could never hope to have men in white helmets and
white armour come to call him. All his ambitions, aims, hope,
and future had been blasted at one fell swoop. The fact that
gossips might spread the news and make him a laughing-stock
for the likes of Young D and Whiskers Wang was only a
secondary consideration.

Never before had he felt so flat. Even coiling his queue on his
head now struck him as pointless and ridiculous. As a form of
revenge he was very tempted to let his queue down at once, but
he did not do so. He wandered about till evening, when after
drinking two bowls of wine on credit he began to feel in better
spirits, and in his mind's eye saw fragmentary visions of white
helmets and white armour once more.

One day he loafed about until late at night. Only when the
tavern was about to close did he start to stroll back to the
Tutelary God's Temple.

Crash-bang!

He suddenly heard an unusual sound, which could not have
been firecrackers. Ah Q, always fond of excitement and of
poking his nose into other people's business, headed straight for
the noise in the darkness. He thought he heard footsteps ahead,
and was listening carefully when a man fled past from the opposite direction. Ah Q instantly wheeled round to follow him.
When that man turned, Ah Q turned too, and when having
turned a corner that man stopped, Ah Q followed suit. He saw
that there was no one after them and that the man was Young
D.

'What's up?' demanded Ah Q resentfully.

'The Zhao . . . Zhao family has been robbed,' panted
Young D.

Ah Q's heart went pit-a-pat. After saying this, Young D
went off. But Ah Q kept on running by fits and starts. However,
having been in the business himself made him unusually bold.
Rounding the corner of a lane, he listened carefully and

thought he heard shouting; while by straining his eyes he
thought he could see a troop of men in white helmets and white
armour carrying off cases, carrying off furniture, even carrying
off the Ningpo bed of the successful county candidate's wife.
He could not, however, see them very clearly. He wanted to go
nearer, but his feet were rooted to the ground.

There was no moon that night, and Weizhuang was very
still in the pitch darkness, as quiet as in the peaceful days of
Emperor Fu Xi.[1] Ah Q stood there until his patience ran out,
yet there seemed no end to the business, distant figures kept
moving to and fro, carrying off cases, carrying off furniture,
carrying off the Ningpo bed of the successful county candidate's
wife . . . carrying until he could hardly believe his own eyes.
But he decided not to go any closer, and went back to the
temple.

It was even darker in the Tutelary God's Temple. When he
had closed the big gate he groped his way into his room, and
only after he had been lying down for some time did he calm
down sufficiently to begin thinking how this affected him. The
men in white helmets and white armour had evidently arrived,
but they had not come to call him; they had taken away fine
things, but there was no share for him—this was all the fault
of the Fake Foreign Devil, who had barred him from the
rebellion. Otherwise how could he have failed to have a share
this time?

The more Ah Q thought of it the angrier he grew, until he
was in a towering rage. 'So no rebellion for me, only for you,
eh?' he fumed, nodding furiously. 'Curse you, you Fake Foreign
Devil—all right, be a rebel! That's a crime for which you get
your head chopped off. I'll turn informer, then see you dragged
off to town to have your head cut off—your whole family
executed. . . . To hell with you!'

[1] One of the earliest legendary monarchs in China.

CHAPTER 9

The Grand Finale

After the Zhao family was robbed most of the people in Weizhuang felt pleased yet fearful, and Ah Q was no exception. But four days later Ah Q was suddenly dragged into town in the middle of the night. It happened to be a dark night. A squad of soldiers, a squad of militia, a squad of police, and five secret servicemen made their way quietly to Weizhuang and, after posting a machine-gun opposite the entrance, under cover of darkness surrounded the Tutelary God's Temple. But Ah Q did not bolt for it. For a long time nothing stirred till the captain, losing patience, offered a reward of twenty thousand cash. Only then did two militiamen summon up courage to jump over the wall and enter. With their co-operation, the others rushed in and dragged Ah Q out. But not until he had been carried out of the temple to somewhere near the machine-gun did he begin to wake up to what was happening.

It was already midday by the time they reached town, and Ah Q found himself carried to a dilapidated yamen where, after taking five or six turnings, he was pushed into a small room. No sooner had he stumbled inside than the door, in the form of a wooden grille, was slammed on his heels. The rest of the cell consisted of three blank walls, and when he looked carefully he saw two other men in a corner.

Although Ah Q was feeling rather uneasy, he was by no means depressed, because the room where he slept in the Tutelary God's Temple was in no way superior to this. The two other men also seemed to be villagers. They gradually fell into conversation with him, and one of them told him that the successful provincial candidate wanted to dun him for the rent owed by his grandfather; the other did not know why he was there. When they questioned Ah Q he answered quite frankly, 'Because I wanted to revolt.'

That afternoon he was dragged out through the grille and taken to a big hall, at the far end of which sat an old man with a cleanly shaven head. Ah Q took him for a monk at first, but when he saw soldiers standing guard and a dozen men in long coats on both sides, some with their heads clean-shaven like this old man and some with a foot of so of hair hanging over their shoulders like the Fake Foreign Devil, all glaring furiously at him with grim faces, he knew that this man must be someone important. At once his knee-joints relaxed of their own accord, and he sank to his knees.

'Stand up to speak! Don't kneel!' shouted all the men in the long coats.

Although Ah Q understood, he felt quite incapable of standing up. He had involuntarily started squatting, improving on this finally to kneel down.

'Slave! . . .' exclaimed the long-coated men contemptuously. They did not insist on his getting up, however.

'Tell the truth and you will receive a lighter sentence,' said the old man with the shaven head in a low but clear voice, fixing his eyes on Ah Q. 'We know everything already. When you have confessed, we will let you go.'

'Confess!' repeated the long-coated men loudly.

'The fact is I wanted . . . to join . . .' muttered Ah Q disjointedly after a moment's confused thinking.

'In that case, why didn't you?' asked the old man gently.

'The Fake Foreign Devil wouldn't let me.'

'Nonsense. It's too late to talk now. Where are your accomplices?'

'What? . . .'

'The gang who robbed the Zhao family that night.'

'They didn't come to call me. They moved the things away themselves.' Mention of this made Ah Q indignant.

'Where are they now? When you have told me I will let you go,' repeated the old man even more gently.

'I don't know. . . . They didn't come to call me. . . .'

Then, at a sign from the old man, Ah Q was dragged back through the grille. The following morning he was dragged out once more.

Everything was unchanged in the big hall. The old man with the clean-shaven head was still sitting there, and Ah Q knelt down again as before.

'Have you anything else to say?' asked the old man gently.

Ah Q thought, and decided there was nothing to say, so he answered, 'Nothing.'

Then a man in a long coat brought a sheet of paper and held a brush in front of Ah Q, which he wanted to thrust into his hand. Ah Q was now nearly frightened out of his wits, because this was the first time in his life that his hand had ever come into contact with a writing-brush. He was just wondering how to hold it when the man pointed out a place on the paper and told him to sign his name.

'I—I—can't write,' said Ah Q, shamefaced, nervously holding the brush.

'In that case, to make it easy for you, draw a circle!'

Ah Q tried to draw a circle, but the hand with which he grasped the brush trembled, so the man spread the paper on the ground for him. Ah Q bent down and, as painstakingly as if his life depended on it, drew a circle. Afraid people would laugh at him, he determined to make the circle round; however, not only was that wretched brush very heavy, but it would not do his bidding. Instead it wobbled from side to side; and just as the line was about to close it swerved out again, making a shape like a melon-seed.

While Ah Q was still feeling mortified by his failure to draw a circle, the man took back the paper and brush without any comment. A number of people then dragged him back for the third time through the grille.

By now he felt not too upset. He supposed that in this world it was the fate of everybody at some time to be dragged in and out of prison and to have to draw circles on paper; it was only his circle not being round that he felt a blot on his escutcheon. Presently, however, he regained composure by thinking, 'Only idiots can make perfect circles.' And with this thought he fell asleep.

That night, however, the successful provincial candidate was unable to sleep, because he had quarrelled with the captain. The successful provincial candidate had insisted that the main thing was to recover the stolen goods, while the captain said the main thing was to make a public example. Recently the captain had come to treat the successful provincial candidate quite disdainfully. So banging his fist on the table he said,

'Punish one to awe one hundred! See now, I have been a member of the revolutionary party for less than twenty days, but there have been a dozen cases of robbery, none of them yet solved; think how badly that reflects on me. Now this one has been solved, you come and haggle. It won't do. This is my affair.'

The successful provincial candidate, most put out, insisted that if the stolen goods were not recovered he would resign immediately from his post as assistant civil administrator.

'As you please,' said the captain.

In consequence the successful provincial candidate did not sleep that night; but happily he did not hand in his resignation the next day after all.

The third time that Ah Q was dragged out of the grille-door was the morning following the night on which the successful provincial candidate had been unable to sleep. When he reached the hall, the old man with the clean-shaven head was sitting there as usual. And Ah Q knelt down as usual.

Very gently the old man questioned him: 'Have you anything more to say?'

Ah Q thought, and decided there was nothing to say, so he answered, 'Nothing.'

A number of men in long coats and short jackets put on him a white vest of foreign cloth with some black characters on it. Ah Q felt most disconcerted, because this was very like mourning dress and to wear mourning was unlucky. At the same time his hands were bound behind his back, and he was dragged out of the yamen.

Ah Q was lifted on to an uncovered cart, and several men in short jackets sat down beside him. The cart started off at once. In front were a number of soldiers and militiamen shouldering foreign rifles, and on both sides were crowds of gaping spectators, while what was behind Ah Q could not see. Suddenly it occurred to him—'Can I be going to have my head cut off?' Panic seized him and everything turned dark before his eyes, while there was a humming in his ears as if he had fainted. But he did not really faint. Although he felt frightened some of the time, the rest of the time he was quite calm. It seemed to him that in this world probably it was the fate of everybody at some time to have his head cut off.

He still recognized the road and felt rather surprised: why were they not going to the execution ground? He did not know that he was being paraded round the streets as a public example. But if he had known, it would have been the same: he would only have thought that in this world probably it was the fate of everybody at some time to be made a public example of.

Then he realized that they were making a detour to the execution ground, so after all he must be going to have his head cut off. He looked round him regretfully at the people swarming after him like ants, and unexpectedly in the crowd by the road-side he caught sight of Amah Wu. So that was why he had not seen her for so long: she was working in town.

Ah Q suddenly became ashamed of his lack of spirit, because he had not sung any lines from an opera. His thoughts revolved like a whirlwind: *The Young Widow at Her Husband's Grave* was not heroic enough. The passage 'Alas, in my cups' in *The Battle of the Dragon and the Tiger* was too feeble. 'Steel mace in hand I shall trounce you' was still the best. But when he wanted to raise his hands, he remembered that they were bound together; so he did not sing 'Steel mace in hand' either.

'In twenty years I shall be another . . .'[1] In his agitation Ah Q uttered half a saying which he had picked up for himself but never used before. 'Good!!!' The roar of the crowd sounded like the growl of a wolf.

The cart moved steadily forward. During the shouting Ah Q's eyes turned in search of Amah Wu, but she did not seem to have seen him for she was looking intently at the foreign rifles carried by the soldiers.

So Ah Q took another look at the shouting crowd.

At that instant his thoughts revolved again like a whirlwind. Four years before, at the foot of the mountain, he had met a hungry wolf which had followed him at a set distance, wanting to eat him. He had nearly died of fright, but luckily he happened to have a knife in his hand which gave him the courage to get back to Weizhuang. He had never forgotten

---

[1] 'In twenty years I shall be another stout young fellow' was a phrase often used by criminals before execution to show their scorn of death. Believing in transmigration, they thought that after death their souls would enter other living bodies.

that wolf's eyes, fierce yet cowardly, gleaming like two will-o'-
the-wisps, as if boring into him from a distance. Now he saw
eyes more terrible even than the wolf's: dull yet penetrating
eyes that having devoured his words still seemed eager to
devour something beyond his flesh and blood. And these eyes
kept following him at a set distance.

These eyes seemed to have merged into one, biting into his
soul.

'Help, help!'

But Ah Q never uttered these words. All had turned black
before his eyes, there was a buzzing in his ears, and he felt as
if his whole body were being scattered like so much light dust.

As for the after-effects of the robbery, the most affected was
the successful provincial candidate, because the stolen goods
were never recovered. All his family lamented bitterly. Next
came the Zhao household; for when the successful county
candidate went into town to report the robbery, not only did
he have his queue cut off by bad revolutionaries, but he had to
pay a reward of twenty thousand cash into the bargain; so all
the Zhao family lamented bitterly too. From that day forward
they gradually assumed the air of the survivors of a fallen
dynasty.

As for any discussion of the event, no question was raised in
Weizhuang. Naturally all agreed that Ah Q had been a bad
man, the proof being that he had been shot; for if he had not
been bad, how could he have been shot? But the consensus of
opinion in town was unfavourable. Most people were dissatisfied, because a shooting was not such a fine spectacle as a
decapitation; and what a ridiculous culprit he had been too, to
pass through so many streets without singing a single line from
an opera. They had followed him for nothing.

December 1921

The White Light   白　光

It was afternoon before Chen Shicheng came back from seeing
the results of the county examinations. He had gone very early,
and the first thing he looked for on the list was the name Chen.
Quite a few Chens leapt to meet his eye, but none followed by
the characters Shicheng. Thereupon, starting again, he made
a careful search through all twelve lists. Even after everyone
else had left, the name Chen Shicheng had not appeared on the
list but the man was still standing there, a solitary figure before
the front wall of the examination school.

A cool wind was ruffling his short greying hair and the early
winter sun shone warmly on him, yet he felt dizzy as if from a
touch of the sun. His pale face grew even paler; his tired eyes,
puffy and red, glittering strangely. In fact, he had long stopped
seeing the results on the wall, for countless black circles were
swimming past his eyes.

He had won his first degree in the county examination and
taken his second in the provincial capital, success following
success. . . . The local gentry were trying by every means to
ally with him by marriage; people were treating him like a god,
cursing themselves for their former contempt and blindness. . . .
The other families renting his tumble-down house had been
driven away—no need for that, they would move of their own
accord—and the whole place was completely renovated with
flagpoles and a placard at the gate. . . . If he wanted to keep
his hands clean he could be an official in the capital, otherwise
some post in the provinces would prove more lucrative. . . .
Once more the future mapped out so carefully had crashed in
ruins like a wet sugar-candy pagoda, leaving nothing but
debris behind.

Not knowing what he did, he turned with a strange sensation of disintegration, and shambled disconsolately home.

The moment he reached his door, seven small boys raised their voices to drone their lesson together. He started as if a chime had been struck by his ear, aware of seven heads with seven small queues bobbing in front of him, bobbing all over the room, with black circles dancing between. As he sat down they handed in their homework, contempt for him manifest on every face.

'You may go,' he said painfully after a brief hesitation.

They snatched up their satchels, stuffed them under their arms, and were off like a streak of smoke.

Chen Shicheng could still see a host of small heads dotted with black circles dancing in front of him, now higgledy-piggledy, now in strange formations; but by degrees they grew fewer, hazier.

'Failed again!'

With a violent start he leapt to his feet, for undoubtedly the sound came from just beside him. When he turned his head there was no one there, yet he seemed to hear another muffled chime and his lips formed the words:

'Failed again!'

Abruptly he raised one hand and reckoned it up on his fingers: eleven, thirteen times, counting this year made sixteen, yet not a single examiner had been capable of appreciating good writing, all had been completely blind. It was so pathetic, in fact, that he had to snigger. In a fury he snatched his neatly copied examination essays and poems from their cloth wrapper and started out with them; but in the doorway he was dazzled by the bright light outside, where even the hens were making fun of him. Unable to still the wild pounding of his heart, he slunk back inside again.

He sat down once more, a strange glitter in his eyes. He could see many things, but hazily—his wrecked future, in ruins like a sugar-candy pagoda before him, was looming so large that it blocked all his ways out.

The neighbours' kitchen fires were long since out, their bowls and chopsticks washed, but Chen Shicheng had not started cooking a meal. His tenants knew from years of experience that after he had seen the results of the county examinations their best course was to close their doors early and mind their own business. First all voices were hushed, then one by one lamps were blown out, till nothing was left but the moon slowly climbing the cold night sky.

The deep blue of the sky was like an expanse of sea, while a few drifting clouds looked as if someone had dabbled a piece of chalk in a dish for washing brushes. The moon discharged cold rays of light down upon Chen Shicheng. At first the orb seemed no more than a newly polished iron mirror, but by some mysterious means this mirror projected light through him until he reflected the shadow of the iron moon.

He paced up and down the yard outside his room, his vision clear now, all around him still. But this stillness was abruptly and rudely shattered as in his ear he distinctly heard the urgent whisper:

'Left turn, right turn . . .'

He pricked up his ears and listened intently as the voice repeated more loudly:

'Right turn!'

Now he remembered. This yard was the place, before his family fortunes declined, where he used to come with his grandmother on summer evenings to enjoy the cool. A boy of ten, he would lie on a bamboo couch while his grandmother sat beside him and told him interesting stories. She had it from her own grandmother, she said, that the founder of the Chen family was a man of great wealth who had built this house and buried a vast store of silver here, which some fortunate descendant was bound to find, although so far no one had discovered it. A clue to the hiding place was in this riddle:

> Left turn, right turn, forward, back!
> Gold and silver by the sack!

Chen Shicheng often quietly cudgelled his brains to guess this riddle. Unfortunately he no sooner hit on a solution than he realized that it was wide of the mark. Once he was sure the treasure was under the room rented to the Tang family, but he lacked the courage to dig there and a little later it struck him as most unlikely. As for the vestiges of earlier excavations in his own room, these were signs of his depression over previous failures in the examination, and the sight of them later shamed and embarrassed him.

But this iron light enfolding him today was gently persuasive. And when Chen Shicheng hesitated, the serious proofs it brought forward, backed up by some covert pressure, compelled him to cast his eyes towards his own room again.

A white light, like a round white fan, was flickering in his room.

'So it's here after all!'

With these words he charged like a lion into the room, but once across the threshold he saw no sign of white light, nothing but a dark, shabby room, with some rickety desks half swallowed up in the shadows. He stood there irresolutely till by degrees his vision cleared and the white light reappeared beyond a doubt, broader this time, whiter than sulphurous flames and lighter than morning mist. It was underneath a desk by the east wall.

Chen Shicheng charged like a lion to the door, but when he put out his hand for the hoe behind it he bumped into a dark shadow. He gave an involuntary shiver and hastily lit the lamp, but there was nothing there except the hoe. He moved away the desk and hardly stopping for breath raised four square flagstones. Kneeling, he saw the usual fine yellow sand, and rolling up his sleeves he removed this sand to reveal black earth beneath. Very carefully and quietly he dug down, stroke by stroke. The night was so still, however, that the thudding of his sharp-bladed hoe against the earth was plainly audible.

The pit was over two feet deep yet still no crock had appeared and Chen Shicheng was beginning to lose heart when—*clang!* —he wrenched his wrist as the hoe struck something hard. He dropped his tool and scrabbled in the soil, discovering a large square brick beneath. His heart was throbbing painfully as with infinite care he prised up this brick, disclosing beneath it the same black earth as before. Although he loosened a great deal of earth, it apparently went down and down without end. All of a sudden, however, he struck a small hard object, something round, probably a rusty coin. There were some fragments of broken china too.

Faint and soaked in sweat, Chen Shicheng burrowed desperately. His heart nearly turned over when he struck another strange object shaped somewhat like a horseshoe, but light and brittle in his hands. Having extracted it with infinite care, he picked it up cautiously and studied it intently by the lamp. Blotched and discoloured like a mouldering bone, it bore an incomplete row of teeth on the upper side. He realized that it must be a jaw-bone. This jaw-bone twitched disconcertingly in his hands and gaped as if with laughter. Finally he heard it mutter:

'Failed again!'

An icy shudder went through him. He let it go. The jaw-bone had barely dropped lightly back into the pit before he bounded out into the yard. He stole a glance at his room. The dazzling lamp and supercilious jaw-bone made it strangely terrifying. Averting his eyes in fear, he lay down in the shadows of the eaves some distance away, where he felt slightly safer. But another sly whisper sounded through the stillness in his ear:

'Not here . . . Go to the hills. . . .'

Chen Shicheng had a faint recollection of hearing this remark in the street that day, and at once light dawned on him. He threw back his head to look up at the sky. The moon was hiding itself behind West Peak, so that the peak a dozen miles from the town seemed immediately before him, upright, black, and awesome as the tablet carried by ministers to court, while from it pulsed great flickering beams of white light.

And this white light in the distance seemed just before him.

'Yes, to the hills!'

This decision taken, he rushed wildly out. Doors banged as he opened them, then all was still. The lamp, its wick heavily furred, lit up the empty room and the gaping pit. Presently it sputtered a few times and by degrees dwindled and died as the oil burned out.

'Open the gate! . . .'

In the dawn this cry, fearful and despairing yet fraught with infinite hope, throbbed and trembled like a floating thread before the West Gate of the town.

At noon the next day someone noticed a drowned man

floating in Wanliu Lake five miles from the West Gate. He lost no time in spreading the news till word reached the local bailiff, who got some villagers to recover the corpse. Is was the body of a man in his fifties, 'of medium height, pale and beardless', completely naked. It may have been Chen Shicheng. But since none of his neighbours could be troubled to go and look and no kinsmen went to identify and claim him, after the county authorities had held an inquest the bailiff buried him. The cause of death was beyond dispute and the theft of a dead man's clothes a common occurrence, insufficient grounds for suspicion of foul play. In fact, the post-mortem established that he had fallen in while still alive, for he had undoubtedly struggled under the water—embedded under all his nails was mud from the bottom of the lake.

June 1922

In the Tavern   在 酒 楼 上

During my travels from the north to the south-east I made a
detour to my home and then went on to S——. This town, only
ten miles from my native place, can be reached in less than half
a day by a small boat. I had taught for a year in a school here.
In the depth of winter after snow the landscape was bleak; but
a combination of indolence and nostalgia made me put up
briefly in the Lo Si Hotel, a new hotel since my time. The town
was small. I looked for several old colleagues I thought I might
find, but not one of them was there. They had long since gone
their different ways. And when I passed the gate of the school
that too had changed its name and appearance, making me
feel quite a stranger. In less than two hours my enthusiasm had
waned and I rather reproached myself for coming.

The hotel I was in let rooms but did not serve meals, which
had to be ordered from outside, but these were about as un-
palatable as mud. Outside the window was only a stained and
spotted wall, covered with withered moss. Above was the leaden
sky, a colourless dead white; moreover a flurry of snow had
begun to fall. Since my lunch had been poor and I had nothing
to do to while away the time, my thoughts turned quite naturally to a small tavern I had known well in the past called One
Barrel House, which I reckoned could not be far from the hotel.
I immediately locked my door and set out to find it. Actually,
all I wanted was to escape the boredom of my stay, not to do
any serious drinking. One Barrel House was still there, its
narrow mouldering front and dilapidated signboard unchanged. But from the landlord down to the waiters there was
not a soul I knew—in One Barrel House too I had become a
complete stranger. Still I climbed the familiar stairway in the
corner to the little upper storey. The five small wooden tables

up here were unchanged; only the window at the back, origi-
ally latticed, had been fitted with glass panes.

'A catty of yellow wine. To go with it? Ten pieces of fried
beancurd with plenty of chilli sauce.'

As I gave this order to the waiter who had come up with
me I went and sat down at the table by the back window. The
fact that the place was empty enabled me to pick the best seat,
one with a view of the deserted garden below. Most likely this
did not belong to the tavern. I had looked out at it many times
in the past, sometimes too in snowy weather. But now, to eyes
accustomed to the north, the sight was sufficiently striking.
Several old plum trees in full bloom were braving the snow as if
oblivious of the depth of winter; while among the thick dark
green foliage of a camellia beside the crumbling pavilion a
dozen crimson blossoms blazed bright as flame in the snow,
indignant and arrogant, as if despising the wanderer's wander-
lust. At this I suddenly remembered the moistness of the heaped
snow here, clinging, glistening, and shining, quite unlike the
dry northern snow which when a high wind blows will fly up to
fill the sky like mist. . . .

'Your wine, sir . . .' said the waiter carelessly, putting down
my cup, chopsticks, wine-pot, and dish. The wine had come. I
turned to the table, set everything straight, and filled my cup.
I felt that the north was certainly not my home, yet when I
came south I could only count as a stranger. The powdery dry
snow which whirled through the air up there and the clinging
soft snow here were equally alien to me. In a slightly melan-
choly mood I took a leisurely sip of wine. The wine tasted pure
and the fried bean curd was excellently cooked, only the chilli
sauce was not hot enough; but then the people of S—— had
never understood pungent flavours.

Probably because it was the afternoon, the place had none
of the atmosphere of a tavern. By the time I had drunk three
cups, the four other tables were still unoccupied. A sense of
loneliness stole over me as I stared at the deserted garden, yet I
did not want other customers to come up. Thus I could not
help being irritated by the occasional footsteps on the stairs,
and was relieved to find it was only the waiter. And so I drank
another two cups of wine.

'This time it must be a customer,' I thought, at the sound of footsteps much slower than those of the waiter. When I judged that he must be at the top of the stairs, I raised my head rather apprehensively to look at this extraneous company and stood up with a start. It had never occurred to me that I might run into a friend here—if such he would still let me call him. The newcomer was an old classmate who had been my colleague when I was a teacher, and although he had changed a great deal I knew him at a glance. Only he had become very slow in his movements, quite unlike the spry dynamic Lu Weifu of the old days.

'Well, Weifu, is that you? Imagine meeting you here!'

'Well, well, is that you? Imagine . . .'

I invited him to join me, but he seemed to hesitate before doing so. This struck me as strange, then I felt rather hurt and annoyed. A closer look revealed that Lu had still the same unkempt hair and beard, but his pale lantern-jawed face was thin and wasted. He appeared very quiet if not dispirited, and his eyes beneath their thick black brows had lost their alertness; but while looking slowly around, at sight of the deserted garden they suddenly flashed with the same piercing light I had seen so often at school.

'Well,' I said cheerfully but very awkwardly, 'it must be ten years since we saw each other. I heard that you were at Jinan, but I was so wretchedly lazy I never wrote. . . .'

'It was the same with me. I've been at Taiyuan for more than two years now with my mother. When I came back to fetch her I learned that you had already gone, gone for good.'

'What are you doing at Taiyuan?' I asked.

'Teaching in the family of a fellow-provincial.'

'And before that?'

'Before that?' He took a cigarette from his pocket, lit it and put it to his lips, then watching the smoke he puffed out said reflectively, 'Just futile work, amounting to nothing at all.'

He in turn asked what I had been doing all these years. I gave him a rough idea, at the same time calling the waiter to bring a cup and chopsticks in order that Lu could share my wine while we had another two catties heated. We also ordered food. In the past we had never stood on ceremony, but now we began deferring to each other so that finally we fixed on four dishes suggested by the waiter: beans spiced with aniseed, jellied pork, fried beancurd, and salted mackerel.

'As soon as I came back I knew I was a fool.' Holding his cigarette in one hand and the wine-cup in the other, he spoke with a bitter smile. 'When I was young, I saw the way bees or flies stuck to one spot. If something frightened them they would buzz off, but after flying in a small circle they would come back to stop in the same place; and I thought this really ridiculous as well as pathetic. Little did I think I'd be flying back myself too after only describing a small circle. And I didn't think you'd come back either. Couldn't you have flown a little further?'

'That's difficult to say. Probably I too have simply described a small circle.' I also spoke with a rather bitter smile. 'But why did you fly back?'

'For something quite futile.' In one gulp he emptied his cup, then took several pulls at his cigarette and his eyes widened a little. 'Futile—but you may as well hear about it.'

The waiter brought up the freshly heated wine and dishes and set them on the table. The smoke and the fragrance of fried beancurd seemed to make the upstairs room more cheerful, while outside the snow fell still more thickly.

'Perhaps you knew,' he went on, 'that I had a little brother who died when he was three and was buried in the country here. I can't even remember clearly what he looked like, but I've heard my mother say he was a very lovable child and very fond of me. Even now it brings tears to her eyes to speak of him. This spring an elder cousin wrote to tell us that the ground beside his grave was gradually being swamped, and he was afraid before long it would slip into the river: we should go at once and do something about it. This upset my mother so much that she couldn't sleep for several nights—she can read letters herself, you know. But what could I do? I had no money, no time: there was nothing that could be done.

'Now at last, because I'm on holiday over New Year, I've been able to come south to move his grave.' He tossed off another cup of wine and looking out of the window exclaimed: 'Could you find anything like this up north? Blossom in thick snow, and the soil beneath the snow not frozen. So the day

9

before yesterday I bought a small coffin in town—because I reckoned that the one under the ground must have rotted long ago—took cotton and bedding, hired four workmen, and went into the country to move his grave. I suddenly felt most elated, eager to dig up the grave, eager to see the bones of the little brother who had been so fond of me: this was a new experience for me. When we reached the grave, sure enough, the river was encroaching on it and the water was less than two feet away. The poor grave not having had any earth added to it for two years was subsiding. Standing there in the snow, I pointed to it firmly and ordered the workmen: "Dig it up."

'I really am a commonplace fellow. I felt that my voice at this juncture was rather unnatural, and that this order was the greatest I had given in all my life. But the workmen didn't find it strange in the least, and set to work to dig. When they reached the enclosure I had a look, and sure enough the coffin had rotted almost completely away: there was nothing left but a heap of splinters and chips of wood. My heart beat faster as I set these aside myself, very carefully, wanting to see my little brother. However, I was in for a surprise. Bedding, clothes, skeleton, all had gone!

'I thought: "These have all disappeared, but hair, I have always heard, is the last thing to rot. There may still be some hair." So I bent down and searched carefully in the mud where the pillow should have been, but there was none. Not a trace remained.'

I suddenly noticed that the rims of his eyes were rather red, but immediately attributed this to the effect of the wine. He had scarcely touched the food but had been drinking incessantly and must have drunk more than a catty; his looks and gestures had become more animated, more like the Lu Weifu whom I had known. I called the waiter to heat two more catties of wine, then turned back to face my companion, my cup in my hand, as I listened to him in silence.

'Actually there was really no need to move it: I had only to level the ground, sell the new coffin, and make an end of the business. Although it might have seemed odd my going to sell the coffin, if the price were low enough the shop from which I bought it would have taken it, and I could at least have recouped a few cents for wine. But I didn't. I still spread out the bedding, wrapped up in cotton some of the clay where his body had been, covered it up, put it in the new coffin, moved it to my father's grave, and buried it beside him. And having a brick vault built kept me busy most of yesterday too, supervising the work. But in this way I can count the affair ended, or nearly enough to deceive my mother and set her mind at rest. Well, well, the look you're giving me shows you are wondering why I've changed so much. Yes, I still remember the time when we went together to the Tutelary God's Temple to pull off the idols' beards, and how for days on end we used to discuss methods of reforming China until we even came to blows. But this is how I am now, willing to let things slide and to compromise. Sometimes I think: "If my old friends were to see me now, probably they would no longer acknowledge me as a friend." But this is what I am like now.'

He took out another cigarette, put it to his lips, and lit it.

'Judging by your expression, you still expect something of me. Naturally I am much more obtuse than before, but I'm not completely blind yet. This makes me grateful to you, at the same time rather uneasy. I'm afraid I've let down the old friends who even now still wish me well. . . .' He stopped and took several puffs at his cigarette before going on slowly: 'Only today, just before coming to this One Barrel House, I did something futile yet something I was glad to do. My former neighbour on the east side was called Zhang Fu. He was a boatman and had a daughter named Ashun. When you came to my house in those days you may have seen her but you certainly wouldn't have paid any attention to her, because she was still small then. She didn't grow up to be pretty either, having just an ordinary thin oval face and pale skin. Only her eyes were unusually large, with very long lashes and whites as clear as a cloudless night sky—I mean the cloudless sky of the north on a windless day; here it is not so clear. She was very capable. She lost her mother while in her teens, and had to look after a small brother and sister besides waiting on her father; and all this she did very competently. She was so economical too that the family gradually grew better off. There was scarcely a neighbour who didn't praise her, and even Zhang Fu often expressed his appreciation. When I was setting off on my journey this time, my mother remembered her—old people's memories are so long. She recalled that once Ashun saw someone wearing red velvet flowers in her hair, and wanted a spray for herself. When she couldn't get one she cried nearly all night, so that her father beat her and her eyes remained red and swollen for two or three days. These red flowers came from another province and couldn't be bought in S——, so how could she ever hope to have any? Since I was coming south this time, my mother told me to buy two sprays for her.

'Far from feeling vexed at this commission, I was actually delighted, really glad of the chance to do something for Ashun. The year before last I came back to fetch my mother, and one day when Zhang Fu was at home I dropped in for some reason to chat with him. By way of refreshment he offered me some buckwheat mush, remarking that they added white sugar to it. As you can see, a boatman who could afford white sugar was obviously not poor and must eat pretty well. I let myself be persuaded but begged them to give me only a small bowl. He quite understood and instructed Ashun: "These scholars have no appetite. Give him a small bowl, but add more sugar." However when she had prepared the concoction and brought it in it gave me quite a turn, because it was a large bowl, as much as I could eat in a whole day. Though compared with Zhang Fu's bowl, admittedly, it was small. This was the first time I had eaten buckwheat mush, and I just could not stomach it though it was so sweet. I gulped down a few mouthfuls and had decided to leave the rest when I happened to notice Ashun standing some distance away in one corner of the room, and I simply hadn't the heart to put down my chopsticks. In her face I saw both hope and fear—fear presumably that she had prepared it badly, and hope that we would find it to our liking. I knew that if I left most of my bowl she would feel very disappointed and sorry. I made up my mind to it and shovelled the stuff down, eating almost as fast as Zhang Fu. That taught me how painful it is forcing oneself to eat; and I remembered experiencing the same difficulty as a child when I had to finish a bowl of worm-medicine mixed with brown sugar. I didn't hold it against her though, because her half-suppressed smile of

satisfaction when she came to take away our empty bowls more
than repaid me for all my discomfort. So that night, although
indigestion kept me from sleeping well and I had a series of
nightmares, I still wished her a lifetime of happiness and hoped
that for her sake the world would change for the better. But
such thoughts were only the residue of my old dreams. The next
instant I laughed at myself, and promptly forgot them.

'I hadn't known before that she had been beaten on account
of a spray of velvet flowers, but when my mother spoke of it I
remembered the buckwheat mush incident and became un-
accountably diligent. First I made a search in Taiyuan, but
none of the shops had them. It was only when I went to
Jinan . . .'

There was a rustle outside the window as a pile of snow
slithered off the camellia which had been bending beneath its
weight; then the branches of the tree straightened themselves,
flaunting their thick dark foliage and blood-red flowers even
more clearly. The sky had grown still more leaden. Sparrows
were twittering, no doubt because dusk was falling and finding
nothing to eat on the snow-covered ground they were going
back early to their nests to sleep.

'It was only when I went to Jinan . . .' He glanced out of
the window then turned back, drained a cup of wine, took
several puffs at his cigarette, and went on, 'Only then did I
buy the artificial flowers. I didn't know whether they were the
same as those she had been beaten for, but at least they were
made of velvet. And not knowing whether she liked deep or
light colours, I bought one spray of red, one spray of pink, and
brought them both here.

'This afternoon right after lunch I went to see Zhang Fu,
having stayed on an extra day just for this. Though his house
was still there it seemed to me rather gloomy, but perhaps that
was simply my imagination. His son and second daughter
Azhao were standing at the gate. Both of them had grown.
Azhao is quite unlike her sister, she looks a fright; but at my
approach she rushed into the house. I learned from the boy that
Zhang Fu was not at home. "And your elder sister?" I asked. At
that he glared at me and demanded what my business with her
was. He looked fierce enough to fling himself at me and bite me.

I dithered, then walked away. Nowadays I just let things slide. . . .

'You can have no idea how I dread calling on people, much more so than in the old days. Because I know what a nuisance I am, I am even sick of myself; so, knowing this, why inflict myself on others? But since this commission had to be carried out, after some reflection I went back to the firewood shop almost opposite their house. The proprietor's mother old Mrs. Fa was still there and, what's more, still recognized me. She actually asked me into the shop to sit down. After the usual polite preliminaries I told her why I had come back to S—— and was looking for Zhang Fu. I was taken aback when she sighed:

' "What a pity Ashun hadn't the luck to wear these velvet flowers."

'Then she told me the whole story. "It was probably last spring that Ashun began to look pale and thin. Later she had fits of crying, but if asked why she wouldn't say. Sometimes she even cried all night until Zhang Fu couldn't help losing his temper and swearing at her for carrying on like a crazy old maid. But when autumn came she caught a chill, then she took to her bed and never got up again. Only a few days before she died she confessed to Zhang Fu that she had long ago started spitting blood and perspiring at night like her mother. But she hadn't told him for fear of worrying him. One evening her uncle Zhang Geng came to demand a loan—he was always sponging on them—and when she wouldn't give him any money he sneered: 'Don't give yourself airs; your man isn't even as good as me!' That upset her, but she was too shy to ask any questions and could only cry. As soon as Zhang Fu knew this, he told her what a decent fellow the husband chosen for her was; but it was too late. Besides, she didn't believe him. 'It's a good thing I'm already this way,' she said. 'Now nothing matters any more.' "

'Old Mrs. Fa also said, "If her man really hadn't been as good as Zhang Geng, that would have been truly frightful. Not the equal of a chicken thief—what sort of creature would that be? But I saw him with my own eyes at the funeral: dressed in clean clothes and quite presentable. And he said with tears in

his eyes that he'd worked hard all those years on the boat to
save up money to marry, but now the girl was dead. Obviously
he was really a good sort, and Zhang Geng had been lying. It
was too bad that Ashun believed such a rascally liar and died
for nothing. Still, we can't blame anyone else: this was Ashun's
fate."

'Since that was the case, my business was finished too. But
what about the two sprays of artificial flowers I had brought
with me? Well, I asked her to give them to Azhao. This
Azhao had fled at the sight of me as if I were a wolf or monster; I really didn't want to give them to her. However, give
them I did, and I have only to tell my mother that Ashun was
delighted with them and that will be that. Who cares about
such futile affairs anyway? One only wants to muddle through
them somehow. When I have muddled through New Year I
shall go back to teaching the Confucian classics.'

'Is that what you're teaching?' I asked in astonishment.

'Of course. Did you think I was teaching English? First I had
two pupils, one studying the *Book of Songs*, the other Mencius.
Recently I have got another, a girl, who is studying the
Canon for Girls.[1] I don't even teach mathematics; not that I
wouldn't teach it, but they don't want it taught.'

'I could really never have guessed that you would be teaching
such books.'

'Their father wants them to study these. I'm an outsider, it's
all the same to me. Who cares about such pointless matters
anyway? There's no need to take them seriously. . . .'

His whole face was scarlet as if he were quite drunk, but the
gleam in his eyes had died down. I gave a slight sigh, not
knowing what to say. There was a clatter on the stairs as several
customers came up. The first was short, with a round bloated
face; the second was tall, with a conspicuous red nose. Behind
them followed others, and as they walked up the small upper
floor shook. I turned to Lu Weifu who was trying to catch my
eye, then called for the bill.

'Is your salary enough to live on?' I asked as we prepared
to leave.

---

[1] A book describing the feudal standard of behaviour for girls and the virtues
they should cultivate.

'I have twenty dollars a month, not quite enough to manage on.'

'What are your future plans then?'

'Future plans? I don't know. Just think: Has any single thing turned out as we hoped of all we planned in the past? I'm not sure of anything now, not even of what tomorrow will bring, not even of the next minute. . . .'

The waiter brought up the bill and handed it to me. Lu Weifu had abandoned his earlier formality. He just glanced at me, went on smoking, and allowed me to pay.

We left the tavern together, parting at the door because our hotels lay in opposite directions. As I walked back alone to my hotel, the cold wind buffeted my face with snowflakes, but I found this thoroughly refreshing. I saw that the sky, already dark, had interwoven with the houses and streets in the white, shifting web of thick snow.

16 February 1924

Leaving the Pass 出 关

Lao Zi[1] was seated motionless, like a senseless block of wood.

'Master, Kong Qiu[2] is here again!' whispered his disciple Gengsang Chu, entering in some annoyance.

'Ask him in. . . .'

'How are you, master?' inquired Confucius, bowing respectfully.

'As always,' replied Lao Zi. 'And you? Have you read all the books in our collection?'

'Yes. But. . . .' For the first time Confucius appeared a little flustered. 'I have studied the Six Classics: *Book of Songs*, *Book of History*, *Book of Ritual*, *Book of Music*, *Book of Change*, and *Spring and Autumn Annals*. To my mind, after all this time, I have mastered them thoroughly. I have been to see seventy-two princes, none of whom would take my advice. It is certainly hard to make oneself understood. Or is it perhaps the Way that is hard to explain?'

'You are lucky not to have met an able ruler,' replied Lao Zi. 'The Six Classics are the beaten track left by the kings of old. How can they blaze a new trail? Your words are like a track which is trodden out by sandals—but sandals are not the same as a path.' After a pause he proceeded: 'White herons have only to gaze fixedly at each other, and the female conceives. With insects, the male calls from windward, the female responds from leeward, and she is impregnated. With hermaphrodites, one creature has a double sex and fecundates itself. Nature cannot be altered, destiny cannot be changed; time cannot be halted,

---

[1] An early Chinese philosopher, founder of the 'do nothing' school of thought. He was a citizen of the kingdom of Chu in the Spring and Autumn Period.

[2] Confucius.

the Way cannot be obstructed. If you have the Way, all things are possible; if you lose it, nothing is possible.'

Like one clubbed over the head, Confucius sat there as if his spirit had departed, to all intents a senseless block of wood.

Eight minutes or so passed. He inhaled deeply and stood up to take his leave, having thanked the master as usual most courteously for his instructions.

Lao Zi did not detain him. He stood up and, leaning on his stick, saw him to the library gate. Not till Confucius was about to mount his carriage did the old man murmur mechanically:

'Must you go? Won't you have some tea? . . .'

'Thank you.'

Confucius mounted his carriage. Leaning against the horizontal bar, he raised his clasped hands respectfully in farewell. Ran You[1] cracked the whip in the air and cried: 'Gee-up!' The carriage rolled off. When it had gone more than ten yards, Lao Zi went back to his room.

'You seem in good spirits today, master.' Gengsang Chu stood beside him, arms at his side, when Lao Zi regained his seat. 'You made quite a speech. . . .'

'Just so,' rejoined Lao Zi wearily with a faint sigh. 'I said too much.' A thought struck him. 'Tell me, what happened to the wild goose that Kong Qiu gave me? Has it been dried and salted? If so, steam it and eat it. I have no teeth anyway, so it's no use to me.'

Gengsang Chu went out. Lao Zi, quiet once more, closed his eyes. All was still in the library but for the sound of a bamboo pole scraping against the eaves as Gengsang Chu took down the dried goose hanging there.

Three months went by. Lao Zi was seated motionless, as before, like a senseless block of wood.

'Master! Kong Qiu is back again!' whispered his disciple Gengsang Chu, entering in some surprise. 'He hasn't been here for so long, I wonder what this visit means. . . .'

'Ask him in. . . .' As usual, Lao Zi said no more than this.

'How are you, master?' inquired Confucius, bowing respectfully.

[1] A disciple of Confucius.

'As always,' replied Lao Zi. 'I have not seen you for a long time. No doubt you have been studying hard in your lodgings?'

'Not at all,' disclaimed Confucius modestly. 'I stayed indoors thinking. I begin to gain a glimmer of understanding. Crows and magpies peck each other; fish moisten one another with their saliva; the sphex changes into a different insect; when a younger brother is conceived, the elder cries. How can I, long removed from the cycle of transformations, succeed in transforming others? . . .'

'Quite so,' said Lao Zi. 'You have attained understanding.'

No further word was said. They might have been two senseless blocks of wood.

Eight minutes or so passed. Confucius inhaled deeply and stood up to take his leave, having thanked the master as usual most courteously for his instructions.

Lao Zi did not detain him. He stood up and, leaning on his stick, saw him to the library gate. Not till Confucius was about to mount his carriage did the old man murmur mechanically:

'Must you go? Won't you have some tea? . . .'

'Thank you!'

Confucius mounted his carriage. Leaning against the horizontal bar, he raised his clasped hands respectfully in farewell. Ran You cracked the whip in the air and cried: 'Gee-up!' The carriage rolled off. When it had gone more than ten yards, Lao Zi went back to his room.

'You seem in low spirits today, master.' Gengsang Chu stood beside him, arms at his side, when Lao Zi regained his seat. 'You said very little. . . .'

'Just so,' rejoined Lao Zi wearily with a faint sigh. 'But you don't understand. I believe I ought to leave.'

'Why?' If a thunderbolt had struck from the blue Gengsang Chu could not have been more astounded.

'Kong Qiu understands my ideas. He knows I'm the only one able to see through him, and this must make him uneasy. If I don't go, it may be awkward. . . .'

'But doesn't he belong to the same Way? Why should you go?'

'No.' Lao Zi waved a dissenting hand. 'Ours is not the same

Way. We may wear the same sandals, but mine are for travel-ling the deserts,[1] his for going to the court.'

'After all, you are his master!'

'Are you still so naïve after all these years with me?' Lao Zi chuckled. 'How true it is that nature cannot be altered, destiny cannot be changed! You should know that Kong Qiu is not like you. He will never come back nor ever call me master again. He will refer to me as "that old fellow", and play tricks behind my back.'

'I could never have thought it. But you are always right, master, in your judgement of men. . . .'

'No, at the beginning I also often made mistakes.'

'Well, then,' continued Gengsang Chu after some thought, 'we'll fight it out with him. . . .'

Lao Zi chuckled again and opened his mouth wide.

'Look! How many teeth have I left?'

'None.'

'What about my tongue?'

'That's still there.'

'Do you understand?'

'Do you mean, master, that what is hard goes first while what is soft lasts on?'

'Precisely. I think you had better pack up your things and go home to your wife. But first groom my dark ox and sun the saddle and saddle-cloth. I shall want them first thing tomorrow.'

On nearing Hangu Pass,[2] instead of taking the highway which led there directly, Lao Zi reined in his ox and turned into a byway to make a slow circuit of the wall. He hoped to scale it. The wall was not too high, and by standing on the ox's back he could just have heaved himself over. But that would have meant leaving the ox inside. To get it across would have needed a crane, and neither Lu Ban[3] nor Mo Di[4] was born at

[1] The deserts in north-western China.

[2] A strategic pass through which the men of ancient times travelled to China's north-west.

[3] Also known as Gongshu Pan; skilful artisan and inventor of the state of Lu.

[4] The ancient Chinese philosopher Mo Di, who founded the Moist school, was a militant opponent of aggressive war. His followers wrote works on defensive military engineering that were attributed to them.

this time, while Lao Zi himself was incapable of imagining such a contraption. In brief, hard as he racked his philosopher's brain, he could think of no way out.

Little did he know that when he turned into the byway he had been spotted by a scout, who promptly reported the fact to the warden of the pass. He had only gone a little more than twenty yards when a troop of horsemen came galloping after him. At the head rode the scout, after him the warden of the pass, Xi, followed by four constables and two customs officers.

'Halt!' several of them shouted.

Lao Zi hastily reined in his dark ox, motionless as a senseless block of wood.

'Well, well!' exclaimed the astonished warden, having rushed forward and seen who it was. He leaped down from his saddle and bowed in greeting. 'I was wondering who it could be. So it's Lao Dan,[1] the chief librarian. This *is* a surprise.'

Lao Zi made haste to clamber off his ox. He peered at the warden through narrowed eyes, saying uncertainly: 'My memory is failing . . .'

'Of course. Quite natural. You wouldn't remember me. I am Warden Xi. I called on you some time ago, sir, when I went to the library to look up *The Essence of Taxation*. . . .'

Meanwhile the customs officers were rummaging through the saddle and saddle-cloth. One pierced a hole with his awl and poked a finger in to feel around. Then he strode off in silence with a look of disdain.

'Are you out for a ride round the wall?' asked Warden Xi.

'No. I was thinking of going out for a change of air. . . .'

'Very good. Very good indeed. Nowadays all the talk is of hygiene. Hygiene is of paramount importance. But this is such a rare opportunity for us, we must beg you to stay in the customs house for a few days so that we may benefit by your instructions. . . .'

Before Lao Zi could reply, the four constables pressed forward and lifted him on to the ox. One of the customs officers pricked the creature's rump with his awl, and the ox, drawing in its tail, made off at a run towards the pass.

[1] i.e., Lao Zi.

Once there, they opened up the main hall to receive him.
This was the central room of the gate-tower and from its
windows nothing could be seen but the loess plateau outside,
sloping down towards the horizon. The sky was blue, the air
pure. This imposing fortress reared up from a steep slope, while
to right and left of its gate the ground fell away so that the cart
track through it seemed to run between two precipices. A single
ball of mud would indeed have sufficed to block it.

They drank some boiled water and ate some unleavened
bread. Then, after Lao Zi had rested for a while, Warden Xi
invited him to give a lecture. Since refusal was out of the question, Lao Zi assented readily. All was bustle and confusion as
the audience took seats in the hall. In addition to the eight men
who had brought him in were four more constables, two customs officers, five scouts, one copyist, one accountant, and one
cook. Some of them had brought brushes, knives, and wooden
tablets[1] to take notes.

Lao Zi sat in the middle like a senseless block of wood. After
a deep silence, he coughed a few times and his lips moved
behind his white beard. At once all the others held their breath
to listen intently while he slowly declaimed:

> 'The Way that can be told of is not an Unvarying Way;
> The names that can be named are not unvarying names.
> It was from the Nameless that Heaven and Earth
>   sprang;
> The named is but the mother that rears the ten thousand
>   creatures, each after its kind . . . .'[2]

The listeners looked at each other. No one took notes. Lao
Zi continued:

> 'Truly, "Only he that rids himself forever of desire can
>   see the Secret Essences";
> He that has never rid himself of desire can see only
>   the Outcomes.
> These two things issued from the same mould, but
>   nevertheless are different in name.

[1] Before the invention of paper records were made on bamboo or wooden strips,
and any mistakes in the writing were scraped off with a knife.

[2] These and the following quotations are from *The Way and Its Power*, translated
by Arthur Waley.

The "same mould" we can but call the Mystery,
Or rather the "Darker than any Mystery",
The Doorway whence issued all Secret Essences.'

Signs of distress were apparent on every face. Some seemed not to know where to put their hands and feet. One of the customs officers gave a huge yawn; the copyist fell asleep, letting slip his knives, brushes, and wooden tablets with a crash on to the mat.

Lao Zi did not appear to have noticed; yet he must have done so, for he went into greater detail. But since he had no teeth, his enunciation was not clear; his Shensi accent mixed with that of Hunan confused the sounds 'l' and 'n'; moreover he punctuated all his remarks with 'er'. They understood him no better than before. But now, as he went into greater detail, their distress became more acute.

To keep up appearances, they had to go through with it. But by degrees, some lay down, others sprawled sideways, as each occupied himself with his own thoughts. At last Lao Zi concluded:

'The Sage's way is to act without striving.'

Even when he fell silent, however, no one stirred. Lao Zi waited for a moment, then added:

'Er, that's all.'

At this they seemed to wake from a lengthy dream. After sitting so long, their legs were too numb to get up immediately. But their hearts knew the same joy and astonishment as prisoners to whom an amnesty is declared.

Lao Zi was ushered into a side room and urged to rest. After drinking a few mouthfuls of boiled water he sat there motionless, to all intents a senseless block of wood.

Meanwhile, outside, a heated discussion took place. Before long four representatives came in to see him. The gist of their communication was: Since he had spoken too fast and failed to use the purest standard speech, no one had been able to take any notes. It would be a great pity if no record were left. Hence they begged him to issue some lecture notes.

'Whass all that then? I didna ken what that bloke was blethering about,' cried the accountant in a strange mixture of dialects.

'You ought to write it all out,' said the copyist, talking thick Soochow. 'Once it's written out, you'll not have spoken for nothing.'

Lao Zi did not understand them too well either. But since the other two had put a brush, knife, and wooden tablets down in front of him, he guessed that what they wanted was the text of his lecture. Since refusal was out of the question, he assented readily. As it was late, he promised to start the next morning. Satisfied with the result of these negotiations, the delegation left.

The next day dawned overcast. Lao Zi felt out of sorts but he set to work, eager to leave the pass as soon as possible. And he could not do this without handing in his text. A glance at the pile of wooden tablets made him feel worse.

But without changing countenance, he sat down quietly and started writing. He cast his mind back to what he had said the previous day, and transcribed each sentence as he remembered it. That was before the invention of spectacles, and his dim old eyes, screwed up till they seemed mere slits, were under considerable strain. Stopping only to drink boiled water and eat some unleavened bread, he wrote for a whole day and a half, yet produced no more than five thousand big characters.

'That should do to get me out of the pass,' he thought.

He took cord and threaded the tablets together, dividing them between two strings. Then, leaning on his stick, he went to the warden's office to deliver his manuscript and express his wish to leave immediately.

Warden Xi was most delighted, most appreciative, most sorry to think of his leaving. After trying in vain to keep him a little longer, he assumed a mournful expression and gave his consent, ordering his constables to saddle the dark ox. With his own hands he took from his shelf a package of salt, a package of sesame, and fifteen cakes of unleavened bread. These he put in a white sack previously confiscated, and presented to Lao Zi for the road. He made it clear that this preferential treatment was reserved for senior authors. A younger man would have got ten cakes only.

With repeated thanks, Lao Zi took the sack. He descended from the fortress, accompanied by all the others. At the pass, he

led the ox by the bridle till Warden Xi implored him to mount
it; and after declining politely for some time, he let himself be
persuaded. Having bid farewell, he turned the ox's head and it
plodded slowly down the sloping highway.

Soon the ox was making rapidly off with big strides. The
others watched from the pass. When Lao Zi was seven or eight
yards away they could still see his white hair and yellow gown,
the dark ox and the white sack. Then dust rose covering both
man and beast, turning everything grey. Presently they could
see nothing but yellow dust—all else was lost to sight.

Back in the customs house, the others stretched themselves
as if a load had been taken off their shoulders and smacked their
lips as if they had made a profit. A number of them followed
Warden Xi into his office.

'Is this the manuscript?' asked the accountant, picking up
one string of wooden tablets and turning them over. 'It's neatly
written at any rate. I dare say a purchaser for it could be found
in the market.'

The copyist stepped forward too and read from the first
tablet:

' "The Way that can be told of is not an Unvarying Way!"
. . . Bah! The same old claptrap. It makes your head ache, I'm
sick of the sound. . . .'

'The best cure for a headache is sleep,' said the accountant,
putting the tablet down.

The copyist laughed, then said, 'I shall have to sleep it off.
Frankly, I went expecting to hear about his love affairs. If I'd
known we'd have to sit there for hours in agony listening to all
that mumbo-jumbo, I wouldn't have gone. . . .'

'That's your fault for misjudging your man.' Warden Xi
laughed. 'What love affairs could he have? He's never been in
love.'

'How do you know?' demanded the copyist, surprised.

'Didn't you hear him say, "By inactivity everything can be
activated"? That's your own fault again for going to sleep. The
old man has "ambitions high as the sky and a fate as thin as
paper".[1] When he wants everything to be "activated", he's

[1] A phrase from the famous classical Chinese novel *The Dream of the Red Chamber*.

reduced to "inactivity". If he started loving someone, he'd have to love everyone. So how could he fall in love? How dare he? Look at yourself: you've only to see a girl, pretty or ugly, to make eyes at her as if she were your wife. When you do get married, like our accountant here, you'll probably behave better.'

Outside a wind sprang up. They felt rather chilly.

'But where is the old man going? What does he mean to do?' The copyist seized this chance to change the subject.

'According to him, he's going to the desert,' said Warden Xi caustically. 'He'll never make it. He'll find no salt or flour out there—even water is scarce. When he starts feeling hungry, I've no doubt he'll come back.'

'Then we'll make him write another book.' The accountant brightened. 'But he must go easy on the unleavened bread. We'll tell him the principle has been changed and we are encouraging young writers. We'll just give him five cakes of unleavened bread for two strings of tablets.'

'He may not stand for that. He'll sulk or make a scene.'

'How can he make a scene if he's hungry?'

'I'm just afraid no one will want to read such trash.' The copyist made a gesture with one hand. 'We may not even get back the cost of five cakes. For instance, if what he says is true, our chief should give up his job as warden of the pass. That's the only way to achieve inactivity and become someone really important. . . .'

'Don't worry,' said the accountant. 'Some people will read it. Aren't there plenty of retired wardens and plenty of hermits who haven't yet become wardens? . . .'

Outside a wind sprang up, swirling yellow dust to darken half the sky. The warden glanced towards the door and saw several constables and scouts still standing there, listening to their conversation.

'What are you gaping at?' he shouted. 'Dusk is falling. Isn't this the time when contraband goods are smuggled over the wall? Go and make your rounds!'

The men outside streaked off like smoke. The men inside fell silent. Both copyist and accountant withdrew. Warden Xi dusted his desk with his sleeve, then picked up the two strings of tablets and put them on the shelves piled high with salt, sesame, cloth, beans, unleavened bread, and other confiscated goods.

December 1935

Reminiscences

Dogs, Cats, and Mice 狗 · 猫 。 鼠

Since last year I seem to have heard some people calling me a cat-hater. The evidence, naturally, was my tale 'Rabbits and Cats', and this being a self-confession there was of course nothing to be said—but that worried me not at all. This year, however, I have begun to feel a little anxious. I cannot help scribbling from time to time, and when what I write is published it seldom scratches certain people where they itch but often strikes them on some sensitive spot. If I am not careful I may even offend celebrities and eminent professors or, worse still, some of the 'elders responsible for guiding the youth'. And that would be extremely dangerous. Why so? Because these bigwigs are 'not to be trifled with'. Why are they 'not to be trifled with'? Because they may become so incensed that they publish a letter in a paper announcing: 'See! Don't dogs hate cats? Mr. Lu Xun himself admits to hating cats yet he also advocates beating "dogs that have fallen into the water"!' The subtlety of this 'logic' lies in its use of words from my own mouth to prove me a dog, from which it follows that the statements I make are completely debunked. Even if I say two twos make four, three threes make nine, every single word is wrong. And since they are wrong, it follows naturally that those gentlemen are right when they claim that two twos make seven and three threes a thousand.

I tried to investigate the 'motive' for their animosity. Far be it from me to ape the fashion of those modern scholars who use motive to belittle a work; I was simply trying to clear myself in advance. To my mind, this would have been an easy matter for an animal psychologist, but unfortunately I lacked that special knowledge. Eventually, however, I discovered the

reason in Dr. O. Dähnhardt's *Folk Tales of Natural History*
which tells the following tale. The animals called a meeting on
important business. All the birds, fish, and beasts assembled
with the exception of the elephant. They decided to draw lots
to choose one of their number to fetch him, and this task fell
to the dog. 'How can I find the elephant?' asked the dog. 'I've
never set eyes on him and have no idea what he looks like.'
The others replied, 'That's easy. He has a humped back.' The
dog went off and met a cat, which immediately arched its back;
so he gave it the message and they went back together. But
when he introduced this arched-back cat to the others as the
elephant, they simply laughed at him. That was the start of the
feud between dogs and cats.

Although it is not very long since the Germans came out of
the forests, their learning and art are already most impressive;
even the binding of their books and the workmanship of their
toys cannot fail to please. But this children's tale is really feeble
to offer such a futile reason for a feud. Since the cat did not arch
its back to impose on others or give itself airs, the dog is to
blame for a lack of acumen. Still, this counts as a reason of a
sort. My own dislike of cats is very different.

In fact, no sharp distinction need be drawn between men and
beasts. Although the animal kingdom is by no means as free and
easy as the ancients imagined, there is less tiresome shamming
there than in the world of men. Animals act according to their
nature, and whether right or wrong never try to justify their
actions. Maggots may not be clean, but neither do they claim
to be immaculate. The way vultures and beasts prey on weaker
creatures may be dubbed cruel, but they have never hoisted
the banners of 'justice' and 'right' to make their victims admire
and praise them right up to the time they are devoured. When
man learned to stand upright, that was of course a great step
forward. When he learned to speak, that was another great
step forward. When he learned to write, that was yet another
great step forward. But then degeneration set in, because that
was the beginning of empty talk. Empty talk is not so bad, but
sometimes one may unwittingly say something one doesn't
really mean; in which case, compared with inarticulate beasts,
men should certainly feel ashamed. If there really is a Creator

above who considers all creatures as equal, he may think these
clever tricks of man rather uncalled for, just as in the zoo the
sight of monkeys turning somersaults or female elephants
curtseying, although it often raises a laugh, may at the same
time make us uncomfortable or even sad, so that we think these
uncalled-for tricks might well be dispensed with. However,
being men we have to 'close ranks against outsiders' and try to
justify ourselves as men do, according to the fashion of the
time.

Now as to my antipathy for cats, I consider that I have
ample reason for it, moreover it is open and above-board.
First, a cat is by nature different from other wild creatures
in that whenever it catches a sparrow or mouse instead of
killing its victim outright it insists on playing with it, letting it
go, catching it again, then letting it go again until tiring of this
game it finally eats it. This is very like the bad human pro-
pensity for delighting in the misfortunes of others and spinning
out their torment. Secondly, although cats belong to the same
family as lions and tigers, they are so sycophantic! However,
this may be owing to innate limitations. If cats were ten times
their present size, there is really no knowing how they would
behave. But these arguments may appear thought up on the
spur of the moment, although I believe they occurred to me
earlier on. A sounder explanation perhaps is simply this: their
caterwauling when mating is so drawn out and overdone that
it gets on people's nerves, especially at night when one wants to
read or sleep. At such times I have to retaliate with a long
bamboo pole. When two dogs mate in the street, idlers often
belabour them with sticks. I once saw an etching of this by
Brueghel entitled *Allegorie der Wollust*, showing that such
actions are and always have been common to China and all
other countries.

Ever since that eccentric Austrian scholar Sigmund Freud
advocated psychoanalysis, some of our celebrities and eminent
professors have made use of it in their insinuations, suggesting
that these actions must also perforce be attributed to sexual
desire. Now, passing over the business of beating dogs to consider my beating of cats, this is solely on account of their caterwauling, quite devoid of malice aforethought, for my jealousy

is not yet so inordinate. In these days when everything one does is wrong, I must proclaim this in advance. For instance, human beings too go through quite a lengthy procedure before mating. The new way is to write love-letters, at least one packet if not a whole sheaf; the old way was to 'inquire names', 'send betrothal gifts', kowtow and bow. When the Jiang family of Haichang had a wedding last year in Peking, they devoted three whole days to ceremonial calls and printed a red-covered Wedding Handbook with a preface in which they expatiated: 'Fairly speaking, all ceremonies should be elaborate. If simplicity were our aim, what need would there be for ceremony? . . . Thus all who set store by ceremony can hold up their heads. They should not descend to the level of the common herd who are too low for ceremony.' This did not enrage me, however, because I was not required to attend; and this shows that my hatred of cats is really very easily explained just by that caterwauling so close to my ears. The various ceremonies others indulge in are not the affair of outsiders and don't worry me; but if someone comes and insists on reciting love-letters or bowing and scraping just as I want to read a book or sleep, I have to defend myself with a long bamboo pole too. Then there are people with whom I normally have little to do who suddenly send me a red invitation card to 'the nuptials of our younger sister' or 'our son's wedding', 'craving the honour' of my company or 'soliciting the attendance' of my whole family. I dislike these phrases with their 'sinister implications' which embarrass me unless I spend some money.

However, all this belongs to the recent past. Looking further back, my hatred of cats dates from a time long before I could expound these reasons, when I was perhaps ten years old. The reason I clearly remember was very simple: because cats eat mice—ate my beloved little pet mouse.

In the West, it is said, they are not too fond of black cats. I have no idea how correct this is; but the black cat of Edgar Allan Poe's story is certainly rather fearsome. Japanese cats are adept at becoming spirits, and the cruelty with which these legendary 'cat witches' devour men is even more terrifying. Although China too had 'cat spirits' in ancient times, in recent years we very seldom hear of feline black magic; it seems the old custom has died out and they have turned honest. And yet as a child I felt no goodwill towards cats, which to me had something monstrous about them. It so happened that one summer evening during my childhood I was lying on a small table under the cool shade of a large fragrant oleander tree while my grandmother, seated beside me waving a plantain fan, regaled me with riddles and stories. Suddenly from the fragrant oleander we heard a stealthy scratch of claws and two gleaming eyes descended through the darkness. I gave a start, while my grandmother broke off her tale to tell me a different story about cats.

'Did you know that the cat was the tiger's teacher?' she asked. 'How could a child know that the cat was once the tiger's master? To start with the tiger couldn't do a thing, so he turned to the cat for help. Then the cat taught him how to pounce on, catch, and eat his prey, the way that it caught rats. After these lessons the tiger thought he had mastered all the skills and no other creature was a match for him except his master the cat. If he killed the cat he would be cock of the walk. He made up his mind to it, and started stalking the cat. But the cat knew what he was up to. With one bound it leaped on to a tree, so that all the tiger could do was squat below glaring up. The cat hadn't taught all its skills: it hadn't taught the tiger to climb trees.'

A good thing too, I thought. How lucky that the tiger was so impatient, otherwise a tiger might come crawling down from the fragrant oleander tree. Still this was all most alarming, I had better go indoors to sleep. It had grown darker; a breeze had sprung up, rustling the fragrant oleander leaves, and the mat on my bed must be cool enough for me to lie quietly without tossing and turning.

A room centuries old, dimly lit by a bean-oil lamp, is the happy hunting-ground of rats who scuttle to and fro squeaking, often giving themselves more arrogant airs than 'celebrities and eminent professors'. We kept a cat but it didn't earn its keep. Although my grandmother and other grown-ups complained of the way the rats gnawed through chests and stole food, that was no great crime in my eyes, and no business of mine; besides it was no doubt the big rats who were to blame for these misdeeds, and I would not have them slanderously imputed to my pet mouse. My type of mouse, no larger than a thumb, mostly scurried about the floor and was not too afraid of people. The local name for them was *yinshu*, and they were a different species from the monsters who lived in the roof. In front of my bed were pasted two coloured woodcuts. One, 'The Marriage of Pigsy', consisted almost entirely of long snouts and large ears, and I didn't think much of it. The other, 'The Mouse's Wedding', was quite charming. Every single mouse in it, from the bridegroom and bride down to the best man, bridesmaids, guests, and attendants, had the high cheekbones and slender legs of scholars, although they wore red jackets and green trousers. To my mind, these beloved mice of mine were the only ones capable of conducting such an elaborate ceremony. Nowadays, things are cruder. When I meet a wedding procession in the street, I simply view it as an advertisement for sexual intercourse and pay scant attention. At that time, however, my longing to see a 'mouse's wedding' was so strong that I doubt whether it would have exhausted my patience even if the ceremonies had continued for three nights, as in the case of the Jiang family of Haichang. On the eve of the Lantern Festival I was always reluctant to go to sleep as I waited for that procession to emerge from under my bed. But all I saw were the same few mice wearing no clothes and parading the floor as usual, not attending any wedding apparently. When I could hold out no longer I fell into a disappointed sleep, and when I opened my eyes again another day had dawned—the Lantern Festival. Perhaps when mice marry they do not issue invitations angling for congratulatory gifts, nor even welcome people really eager to watch. This I imagine has always been their way and to protest is useless.

As a matter of fact the great enemy of mice is not the cat. At the end of spring if you hear the squeaking described as 'mice counting coppers' you will know that the Terror of Rats has appeared on the scene. This sound, expressing the panic of despair, is not caused by confrontation with a cat. Although a cat is frightening, mice need only dart into a small hole to render it powerless. They have many chances to escape. Only that baneful butcher the snake, long, thin, and about the same in circumference as a mouse, can go wherever mice go and is so tenacious in pursuit that few mice escape from it. By the time one hears the 'counting of coppers', the mouse is probably doomed.

Once I heard the 'counting of coppers' from an empty room. When I opened the door and went in there was a snake on the beam. Lying on the floor I saw a mouse with blood trickling from one corner of its mouth, but still breathing. I picked it up and put it in a cardboard box where after a long time it came to. By degrees it was able to eat, drink, and crawl about; and by the next day it seemed to have recovered. But it did not run away. When put on the ground it kept running up to people and climbing up their legs, right up to the knee. Placed on the dining table, it would eat left-overs and lick the edges of bowls. Put on my desk, it would wander about freely and lick some of the ink being ground on the ink-stone. This amazed and delighted me. I had heard from my father that China had an ink-monkey no bigger than a thumb, covered with shining jet-black fur. It used to sleep in the jar for writing-brushes. At the sound of ink being ground it would jump out and wait. When the scholar had finished writing and put away his brush, it would lick up all the ink left on the ink-stone, then jump back into the brush jar. I longed, in vain, to possess one of these ink-monkeys. When I asked where they lived or where they could be bought, nobody could tell me. Second-best is better than nothing. This mouse could count as my ink-monkey, although it did not always wait for me to finish writing before licking up my ink.

My recollection is none too clear, but this must have gone on for a month or two before, one day, I suddenly felt as lonely 'as if bereft of something'. My mouse was always in my sight running about on the table or on the floor. But today I hadn't seen it for hours. It didn't even come after the midday meal, a time when it normally always put in an appearance. I waited and waited all the rest of the day—still no sign of my mouse.

Mama Chang, my nurse, may have thought this waiting too upsetting for me, for she padded over to whisper something to me which plunged me into a fit of rage and grief and made me vow eternal hatred to cats. She told me that my mouse had been eaten the night before by the cat.

When I lose something I love, it leaves a gap in my heart which I have to fill in with schemes for revenge.

I set about my vengeance with our tabby, extending it gradually to all cats who crossed my path. To start with I just chased and beat them; later I refined on this and learned to hit them on the head with my sling or lure them into an empty room and belabour them until they were thoroughly chastened. This feud continued for a very long time until finally it seemed no cats came near me. But triumphing over cats most likely does not make a hero of me; moreover there cannot be too many people in China who keep up a life-long feud with cats; hence I will pass over all my stratagems and exploits.

However, many days later, possibly even more than six months later, I happened to receive some unexpected news. My mouse had not been eaten by a cat—it had been trampled to death by Mama Chang when it tried to run up her leg.

This possibility had never occurred to me. I no longer remember my immediate reaction, but I was never reconciled to cats. After I came to Peking, the havoc wreaked among my small rabbits by a cat added to my former animosity, and I took sterner measures of reprisal. That gave a handle to those who call me a cat-hater. But today these are all things of the past and my attitude to cats has changed to one of extreme politeness. If forced to it I simply drive them away, never beating or hurting them let alone killing them. This is a mark of my progress in recent years. Accumulated experience led me to the sudden realization that nine persons out of ten are naturally disgusted by the way cats steal fish and meat, carry off chickens, or caterwaul late at night, and this disgust is centred on the cat. Should I attempt to rid men of this disgust by beating or killing cats, these would instantly become objects of pity while that disgust would be transferred to me. Accordingly my present method is: whenever I find cats making a nuisance of themselves, I step to my doorway and shout, 'Hey! Scram!' When things quieten down a little I return to my study. In this way I preserve my reputation of safeguarding our home against foreign aggression. Actually this method is one com-

monly practised by officers and soldiers in China, who prefer
not to wipe out all brigands or exterminate the enemy completely, for if they did so they would cease to be highly regarded
and might even lose their function and their posts. To my
mind, if I can get more people to use this tactic, I can hope to
become one of the 'elders responsible for guiding the youth'.
But I have not yet decided whether or not to put this into
practice. I am still studying and pondering the matter.

21 February 1926

Ah Chang and the
Book of Hills and Seas[1]

阿 长 与 山 海 经

Mama Chang, as I have said elsewhere, was the maid who brought me up or—to give her a grander title—my nurse. That is what my mother and many others called her, for this sounded a little more polite. Only my grandmother called her 'Ah Chang'. I usually called her 'Amah' without even adding the 'Chang'. But when I was angry with her—upon learning that she was the one who had killed my mouse, for example— then I also called her 'Ah Chang'.

We had no one in our parts with the surname Chang; and since she was swarthy, plump, and short, 'Chang' (long) was not used descriptively either. Nor was it her personal name. I remember she told me her name was Something Girl. What the epithet was I have forgotten, but it certainly was not 'Long'. And I never knew her surname. I recall her once telling me how she came by the name. Many, many years ago, our family had a very tall maidservant who was the real Ah Chang. Later on, when she left, this Something Girl of mine came to take her place; but because everyone was used to the name and did not want to change it, from that time on she became Mama Chang too.

Although it is bad to tell tales behind people's backs, if you want me to speak frankly I must admit I did not think much of her. What I most disliked was her habit of gossiping: she would shake her forefinger up and down in the air, or point to the tip of her hearer's nose or her own. Whenever a minor storm blew up in the house, I could not help suspecting that her tittle-tattle had something to do with it. She restricted my move-

[1] A collection of legends dating from the time of the Warring States (fourth to second century B.C.).

ments too. If I pulled up a weed or turned over a stone, she would say I was naughty and threaten to tell my mother. And in bed during the summer she would stretch out her arms and legs like a huge character 大 (*da*), squeezing me so that I had no room to turn over, and my corner of the matting became hot after much lying on. But I could neither push her over, nor could I wake her by shouting.

'You're so plump, Mama Chang, you must find the heat very trying. Isn't that an awkward position for sleeping in?'

My mother put this question after hearing me complaining many times. And I knew it was a hint to my nurse to leave me more space. Ah Chang did not say anything. But that night when the heat woke me up, there was still a big character 大 spread-eagled over the bed, and one of her arms was thrown across my neck. It seemed to me there was really no way out.

She was most conventional in many ways, however, though most of her customs made me lose patience. The happiest time of the year was naturally New Year's Eve. After seeing the old year out, I put by my pillow the money wrapped in red paper which the grown-ups had given me. The next morning I could spend it as I pleased. I lay on my pillow eyeing the red packages, thinking of the small drum, the weapons, the clay figures, and the sugar Buddha that I would buy tomorrow. Then she came in and put a Good-Luck Orange at the head of the bed.

'Remember this carefully, son!' she told me earnestly. 'Tomorrow's the first day of the first month. When you open your eyes in the morning the first thing you must say is: "Good luck, Amah!" Remember? You must remember, because this decides the whole year's luck. Don't say anything else, mind! And after you've said that, you must eat a piece of Good-Luck Orange.' She picked up the orange and flourished it in front of me. 'Then—

> "The whole year through
> Luck will follow you!"'

Even in my dreams I remembered it was New Year, and the next morning I woke specially early. As soon as I opened my eyes, I wanted to sit up. But at once she put out an arm to stop me. I looked at her in surprise, and saw her gazing at me anxiously.

Appealingly, as it were, she shook my shoulder. And suddenly I remembered.

'Good luck, Amah.'

'Good luck! Good luck to us every one! Clever boy! Good luck!' Absolutely delighted, she laughed as she stuffed something icy cold into my mouth. When I had recovered from the shock, I realized that this must be the Good-Luck Orange. Now that all the ordeals to usher in New Year's Day were safely over, I could get up and play.

She taught me much other lore as well. For instance, if someone died, you should not say he was dead but 'he has passed away'. You should not enter a room where someone had died or a child had been born. If a grain of rice fell to the ground, you should pick it up, and the best thing was to eat it. On no account must you walk under the bamboo pole on which trousers or pants were hanging out to dry. . . . There was more, but I have forgotten most of it; and what I remember most clearly are the strange New Year rites. In short, these were all such niggling trifles that the thought of them today still makes me lose patience.

On one occasion, though, I felt an unprecedented respect for her. She often told me stories about the Long Hairs.[1] And the Long Hairs she described were not only Hong Xiuquan's troops but appeared to include all later bandits and rebels as well, with the exception of the modern revolutionaries, who did not exist then. She described the Long Hairs as most fearful beings who talked in a way that no one could understand. According to her, when the Long Hairs entered our city all my family fled to the seaside, leaving just a gate-keeper and an old woman who did the cooking to look after the property. Then, sure enough, a Long Hair came to our house. The old woman called him 'Great King'—it seems this was the way to address the Long Hairs—and complained that she was starving.

---

[1] The Taiping army of the peasant revolt of 1851–64. After the establishment of the Qing dynasty, Chinese men were forced to shave the hair above their foreheads and wear queues. Since the Taipings kept all their hair, they were called Long Hairs.

'In that case,' said the Long Hair with a grin, 'you can have this to eat!' And he tossed over something round with a small queue still attached to it—it was the gate-keeper's head! The old woman's nerves were never the same again. Whenever people spoke of this later, she would turn the colour of earth and beat her breast. 'Ai-ya!' she would whimper. 'It gave me such a turn! Such a turn it gave me. . . .'

I was not afraid, for I felt all this had nothing to do with me—I was not a gate-keeper. But Ah Chang must have guessed my thoughts, for she said:

'The Long Hairs would carry off little boys like you as well, to make little Long Hairs out of them. They carried off pretty girls too.'

'Well, you'd be all right anyway.'

I was sure she would have been quite safe, for she was neither a gate-keeper, nor a little boy, nor pretty. In fact, she had several scars on her neck where sores had been cauterized.

'How can you say such a thing?' she demanded sternly. 'Were we no use to them then? They would carry us off as well. When government troops came to attack the city, the Long Hairs would make us take off our trousers and stand in a line on the city wall, for then the army's cannon could not be fired. If they fired then, the cannon would burst!'

This was certainly beyond my wildest dreams. I could not but be amazed. I had thought of her as nothing but a repository of irksome conventions, never guessing she had this tremendous spiritual power. After this I felt a special respect for her, for surely she was too deep for me to fathom. If she stretched out her arms and legs at night and occupied the whole bed, that was quite understandable. I ought to make room for her.

Although my respect for her wore off by degrees, I believe it did not disappear completely till I discovered it was she who had killed my mouse. I cross-examined her sternly on that occasion, and called her 'Ah Chang' to her face. Since I was not a little Long Hair and would not attack a city or let off a cannon, I need not be afraid of the cannon exploding—so why, thought I, need I be afraid of her?

But while mourning for my mouse and avenging him, I was also longing for an illustrated copy of the *Book of Hills and Seas*.

This longing had been aroused by a distant great-uncle of ours. A fat and kindly old man, he liked to grow plants such as chloranthus or jasmine, or the rare silk tree which is said to have come from the north. His wife was just the reverse: she had no interest in flowers. Once she broke a branch of chloranthus by propping the bamboo for hanging out clothes on it; but her only reaction was to swear at the branch for breaking. The old man was a lonely soul with no one to talk to, so he liked children's company and often even called us his 'young friends'. In the compound where several branches of our clan lived, he was the only one with many books, and unusual ones at that. He had volumes of the essays and poems written for the examinations, of course; but his was the only study where I could find Lu Ji's [1] *Commentaries on the Flora and Fauna in the Book of Songs*, and many other strange titles. My favourite in those days was *The Mirror of Flowers* [2] with all its illustrations. He told me there was an illustrated edition of the *Book of Hills and Seas* with pictures of man-faced beasts, nine-headed snakes, three-footed birds, men with wings, and headless monsters who used their teats as eyes. . . . Unfortunately, he happened to have mislaid it.

Eager as I was to look at pictures of this kind, I did not like to press him to find the book for me. He was very indolent. And none of the people I asked would give me a truthful answer. I had several hundred coppers of New Year money, but no opportunity to buy that book. The main street where books were sold was a long way from our house, and the New Year holiday was the only time in the year when I was able to go there to look around; but during that period the doors of both bookshops were firmly closed.

As long as I was playing it was not so bad, but the moment I sat down I remembered the illustrated *Book of Hills and Seas*.

Probably because I harped on the subject so much, even Ah Chang started asking what this *Book of Hills and Seas* was. I had never mentioned it to her, for I knew she was no scholar, so telling her would serve no purpose. Since she asked me, however, I told her.

[1] A writer of the third century A.D.
[2] A book on gardening by Chen Haozi of the seventeenth century.

About a fortnight or a month later, as I remember, four or five days after she had gone home on leave, she came back wearing a new blue cloth jacket. The moment she saw me she handed me a package.

'Here, son!' she said cheerfully. 'I've bought you that *Book of Holy Seas* with pictures.'

This was like a thunderbolt. I was struck all of a heap. I hastened to take the package and unwrap the paper. There were four small volumes and, sure enough, when I flipped through the pages, the man-faced beast, the nine-headed snake . . . all of them were there.

This inspired me with a new respect. What others would not or could not do, she had been able to accomplish. She really did have tremendous spiritual power. My resentment against her for killing my mouse vanished for good and all.

These four volumes were the first I ever possessed, and my most treasured book.

I can still see them today. But now it seems to me that both the printing and the engraving were extremely crude. The paper was yellow and the drawings very poor, consisting almost entirely of straight lines joined together—even the animals' eyes were oblong. Nevertheless this was my most treasured book. There you could really find the man-faced beast, the nine-headed snake, the one-footed ox, the sack-like monster Di Jiang, and Xing Tian who had no head but 'used his teats as eyes and his navel as mouth' and 'danced with spear and shield'!

After this I began seriously collecting illustrated books. I acquired the *Phonetics and Illustrations for Er Ya*[1] and *Illustrations to the Book of Songs*.[2] I also had the *Paintings Collected by the Dian Shizhai*[3] and *A Shipload of Painting and Poetry*.[4] I bought another lithographed edition of the *Book of Hills and Seas* too, with illustrations and concluding verses to each chapter. The pictures were green and the characters red—much more handsome than my wood-block edition—and I had this book till the year before last. It was a small edition with Hao Yixing's[5]

---

[1] An ancient Chinese lexicon dating from the second century B.C.
[2] A Japanese book of the eighteenth century.
[3] A collection of the work of Chinese and Japanese painters, printed in 1885.
[4] Ming dynasty paintings.
[5] A Qing dynasty scholar (1757–1825).

commentary. As for the wood-block edition, I cannot remember now when that was lost.

My nurse, Mama Chang or Ah Chang, must have departed this life a good thirty years ago. I never found out her name or history. All I know is that she had an adopted son, so she was probably left a widow very early.

Dark, kindly Mother Earth, may her spirit ever rest peacefully in your bosom!

10 March 1926

The Fair of the Five Fierce Gods

五 猖 会

In addition to New Year and the other festivals, we children looked forward to the temple fairs in honour of certain gods. But because my home was rather out of the way, not till the afternoon did the processions pass our door, by which time the retinue had dwindled away until there was almost nothing left of it. Often, after hours of craning our necks and waiting, all we saw was some dozen men running hastily past carrying an effigy of a god with a golden, blue, or crimson face. And that was all.

I always hoped that *this* procession would be bigger and better than the last, but the result was invariably more or less the same. And all I was left with was a souvenir bought for one copper before the god passed by—a whistle made of a bit of clay, a scrap of coloured paper, a split bamboo, and two or three cock's feathers. This whistle, known as a 'tootle-toot', produced a piercing blast, and I blew it lustily for two or three days.

Now when I read Zhang Dai's [1] *Reminiscences*, I am struck by the splendour of temple fairs in his time, even if these Ming dynasty writers do tend to exaggerate. We still welcome the dragon king today when we pray for rain, but it is very simply done, with only some dozen men carrying a dragon and making it twist and coil, while village boys dress up as sea monsters. In the old days they acted plays, and it was most spectacular. Here is Zhang Dai's description of a pageant with characters from *Heroes of the Marshland*: [2]

[1] A seventeenth-century writer.
[2] The famous fourteenth-century novel *Shui Hu Zhuan* by Shi Naian, describing the peasant revolt of Liangshan in the twelfth century.

. . . They went out in all directions to find one fellow who was short and swarthy, another who was tall and hefty, a mendicant friar, a fat monk, a stout woman and a slender one. They looked for a pale face too and a head set askew, a red moustache and a handsome beard, a strong dark man and one with ruddy cheeks and a long beard. They searched high and low in the town, and if they failed to find any character they went outside the city walls, to the villages and hamlets in the hills, even to neighbouring prefectures and counties. A high price was paid to the thirty-six men who played the heroes of Liangshan; but each looked his part to the life, and they went out in force on horseback and on foot. . . .

Who could resist watching such a lifelike pageant of the men and women of days gone by? The pity is that such brave shows disappeared long ago along with the Ming dynasty.

Though these processions were not prohibited by the authorities—unlike women's long gowns in Shanghai today or the discussion of politics in Peking—still, women and children were not allowed to watch them, and educated people or the so-called literati seldom went to look on either. Only layabouts and idlers would gather before the temple or yamen to watch the fun; and since most of my knowledge of these festivities comes from their accounts it is not the first-hand observation so much valued by researchers.[1] I do, however, remember once witnessing a rather fine show myself. First came a boy on horseback called The Announcer. Then, after a considerable interval, the High Pole arrived. This was a great bamboo pole to which a long banner was attached, and it was carried in both hands by a huge fat man dripping with perspiration. When in the mood he would balance the pole on his head or teeth, or even on the tip of his nose. He was followed by stilt-walkers, children on platforms carried by men, and other children on horseback, all masquerading as characters from operas. There were people dressed in red like felons too, loaded with cangues and chains, some of whom were also children. To me each part was glorious and each participant extremely lucky—I no doubt envied them this chance to show off. I used to wish I could have

[1] An allusion to those reactionary intellectuals who supported the warlords in their repression of progressives and posed as 'upright gentlemen', champions of justice, or scholars dedicated to research work.

some serious illness, so that my mother would go to the temple
to promise the god that I would masquerade as a felon. . . . So
far, though, I have failed to have any association with these
processions.

Once I was to go to Dongguan Village for the Fair of the Five
Fierce Gods. This was a great occasion in my childhood, for
this fair was the grandest in the whole county and Dongguan
Village was very far from my home, more than twenty miles by
boat from the town. There were two remarkable temples there.
One was the Temple to Lady Mei, the virgin mentioned in
the *Tales of Liao Zhai*[1] who remained unmarried after the death
of her betrothed and became a goddess after she died, but then
appropriated someone else's husband. On the shrine, sure
enough, the images of a young man and woman were smiling
at each other, counter to all the laws of propriety. The other
was the Temple of the Five Fierce Gods, the very name of
which was strange enough. According to those with a passion
for research, these were the Wu Tong gods.[2] There is no con-
clusive proof of this, however. The images were five men, who
did not look particularly fierce, and behind them sat five wives
in a row, this intermingling of sexes falling far short of the strict
segregation practised in Peking theatres. In fact, this was
counter to all the laws of propriety too; but since these were the
Five Fierce Gods, nothing could be done about it. They were
obviously an exception to the rule.

Since Dongguan Village was a long way from the town, we
all got up at dawn. The big boat with three windows booked the
night before was already moored in the harbour, and to it our
man started carrying the chairs, food, a stove for brewing tea,
and a hamper of cakes. Laughing and skipping, I urged him
to get a move on. Suddenly from his respectful expression I knew
there was something up. I looked round and saw my father
standing behind me.

'Go and fetch your book,' he said slowly.

The book he meant was the *Rhymed History*[3] which served

---

[1] A collection of short stories by Pu Songling (1640–1715).
[2] Licentious deities worshipped in certain villages in the past.
[3] By Wang Shiyun of the Qing dynasty. This book gave a rhymed account of
Chinese history to the end of the Ming dynasty.

as my primer. I had no other book. In our district children started school when their years were odd not even: that is how I know I must have been seven at the time.

With trepidation I fetched the book. He made me sit beside him at the table in the centre of the hall and read to him sentence by sentence. Inwardly quaking, I read to him sentence by sentence.

Two sentences made one line, and I must have read twenty or thirty lines.

'Learn them by heart,' he said. 'If you cannot recite them correctly, you will not be allowed to go to the fair.'

This said, he stood up and walked into his room.

I felt as if someone had doused me with icy water. But what could I do? Naturally I had to read and re-read, and force myself to memorize—I would have to recite it too.

> In the beginning was Pan Gu,
> Born of primeval void;
> He was the first to rule the world,
> The chaos to divide.

That is the kind of book it was. The first four lines are all I can remember. I have forgotten the rest, including of course the twenty or thirty lines I was forced to memorize that day. I remember hearing it said at the time that studying the *Rhymed History* was more useful than studying the *Thousand Characters* or the *Hundred Surnames*,[1] for from it you could learn the outline of all history past and present. It is naturally a very good thing to know the outline of all history past and present. My trouble was that I could not understand a word.

'In the beginning was Pan Gu,' I read.

> In the beginning was Pan Gu. . . .

I read on and learned it by heart.

> In the beginning was Pan Gu,
> Born of primeval void. . . .

Everything needed had been carried to the boat. The noise and bustle at home had turned to silence. The morning sun

---

[1] Two school primers.

shone on the western wall. The weather was clear and fine. Mother, the servant, my nurse Mama Chang or Ah Chang— none of them could rescue me. They had to wait in silence till I had learned my lesson and could recite it. In the utter stillness it seemed as if iron pincers would thrust out from my head to seize that 'Born of primeval void' and all the other lines. And I could hear my voice quaver as I read desperately on, quaver like a cricket's chirping on a late autumn night.

Everybody was waiting. The sun had risen even higher.

Suddenly I felt a surge of confidence. I stood up, picked up the book, and went to my father's study to recite all those lines in one breath. I recited as if in a dream.

'Good. You may go.' Father nodded his head as he spoke.

At once everyone sprang into action, breaking into smiles as we set out for the harbour. The servant carried me high as if to congratulate me on my success as he strode ahead of the rest.

I was not as happy as they were, though. After the boat cast off, the riverside scenery, the cakes in the hamper, the bustle of the fair when we reached Dongguan Village—none of these seemed to me very interesting.

Now everything else is forgotten, vanished without a trace. Only my recitation from the *Rhymed History* is as clear in my mind as if it happened yesterday.

Even now, when I think of it, I still wonder why my father made me learn a lesson by heart at a time like that.

25 May 1926

Father's Illness   父 亲 的 病

It must be over ten years now since this story of a well-known
doctor was the talk of the town in S——:

He charged one dollar forty a visit, ten dollars for an emergency call, double the amount for a night call, and double
again for a trip outside the city. One night the daughter of
a family living outside the city fell dangerously ill. They sent
to ask him out there and, because he had more money at the
time than he knew what to to with, he refused to go for less
than a hundred dollars. They had to agree to this. Once there,
though, he simply gave the girl a perfunctory looking over.

'It isn't serious,' he said.

Then he made out a prescription, took his hundred dollars,
and left.

Apparently the patient's family were very rich, for the next
day they asked him out there again. The master of the house
met him at the door with a smile.

'Yesterday evening we gave her your medicine, Doctor,' he
said, 'and she's much better. So we've asked you to have
another look at her.'

He took him as before into the bedroom, and a maid drew
the patient's hand outside the bed curtain. The doctor placed
his fingers on the wrist and found it icy cold, without any
pulse.

'Hmm.' He nodded. 'I understand this illness.'

Quite calmly he walked to the table, took out a prescription
form, and wrote on it: 'Pay the bearer one hundred silver
dollars.'

Beneath he signed his name and affixed his seal.

'This illness looks rather serious, Doctor,' said the master of the house, behind him. 'I think the medicine should be a little more potent.'

'Very well,' said the doctor. And he wrote another prescription: 'Pay the bearer two hundred silver dollars.'

Beneath he signed his name and affixed his seal again.

This done, the master of the house put away the prescription and saw him politely out.

I had dealings with this famous physician for two whole years, because he came every other day to attend my father. Although by that time very well known, he had not yet more money than he knew what to do with; still, his fee was already one dollar forty a visit. In large towns today a ten-dollar fee is not considered exorbitant; but in those days one dollar forty was a great sum, by no means easy to raise—especially when it fell due every other day.

He probably *was* unique in some respects. It was generally agreed that his prescriptions were unusual. I know nothing about medicine: what struck me was how hard his 'adjuvants' were to find. Each new prescription kept me busy for some time. First I had to buy the medicine, then look for the adjuvant. He never used such common ingredients as two slices of fresh ginger, or ten bamboo leaves minus the tips. At best it was reed roots, and I had to go to the river to dig them up; and when it came to sugar cane which had seen three years of frost, I would have to search for two or three days at the least. But, strange to say, I believe my quest was always successful in the end.

It was generally agreed that herein lay his skill. There once was a patient whom no drugs could cure, but when he met a certain Dr. Ye Tianshi, all this doctor did was to add phoenix-tree leaves as the adjuvant to the old prescription. After one dose, the patient was cured. Because it was autumn then, and the phoenix tree is the first to feel the approach of autumn, where all other drugs had failed Dr. Ye could now use the spirit of autumn to cure the patient. . . . Although this was not clear to me, I was thoroughly impressed and realized that all efficacious drugs must be difficult to get. Those who want to become immortals even have to risk their lives to go deep into the mountains to pluck the herb of long life.

After two years of his visits, I gradually came to know this famous physician fairly well; indeed we were almost friends. Father's dropsy grew daily worse, till it looked as if he would have to keep to his bed, and by degrees I lost faith in such remedies as sugar cane which had seen three years of frost, and was not nearly as zealous as before in finding and preparing adjuvants. One day just at this time, when the doctor called, after inquiring after my father's illness he told us very frankly:

'I've used all the knowledge I have. There is a Dr. Chen Lianhe here, who knows more than I do. I advise you to consult him. I'll write you a letter. This illness isn't serious, though. It's just that he can cure it much more quickly.'

The whole household seemed rather unhappy that day, but I saw him out as respectfully as ever to his sedan chair. When I went in again, I found my father looking very put out, talking it over with everyone and declaring that there was probably no hope for him. Because this doctor had treated the illness for two years to no purpose, and knew the patient too well, he could not help feeling rather embarrassed now that things had reached a crisis: that was why he had recommended someone else, washing his hands of the whole affair. But what else could we do? It was a fact that the only other well-known doctor in our town was Chen Lianhe. So the next day we engaged his services.

Chen Lianhe's fee was also one dollar forty. But whereas our first well-known doctor's face was plump and round, his was plump and long: this was one great difference between them. Their use of medicine was different too. Our first well-known doctor's prescriptions could be prepared by one person, but no single person could cope satisfactorily with Dr. Chen's because his prescriptions always included a special pill or powder or an extra-special adjuvant.

Not once did he use reed roots or sugar cane that had seen three years of frost. Most often it was 'a pair of crickets', with a note in small characters at the side: 'They must be an original pair, from the same burrow.' So it seems that even insects must be chaste; if they marry again after losing their mates they forfeit even the right to be used as medicine. This task, however, presented no difficulties to me. In Hundred Plant Garden I could catch ten pairs easily. I tied them with a thread and dropped them alive into the boiling pan, and that was that. But then there was 'ten ardisia berries'. Nobody knew what these were. I asked the pharmacy, I asked some peasants, I asked the vendor of herb medicines, I asked old people, I asked scholars, I asked a carpenter: but they all simply shook their heads. Last of all I remembered that distant great-uncle of mine, the old fellow who liked to grow flowers and trees, and hurried over to ask him. Sure enough, he knew: the ardisia was a shrub which grew at the foot of trees deep in the mountain. It had small red berries like coral beads, and was usually known as Never-Grow-Up.

> You wear out iron shoes in hunting round,
> When all the time it's easy to be found!

Now we had the adjuvant, but there was still a special pill: broken-drum bolus. Broken-drum boluses were made from the leather of worn-out drums. Since one name for 'dropsy' is 'drum-tight', the leather from worn-out drums can naturally cure it. Gang Yi of the Qing dynasty, who hated 'foreign devils', acted on the same principle when he prepared to fight them by training a corps of 'tiger angels', for the tigers would be able to eat the sheep,[1] and the angels could subdue the devils. Unfortunately there was only one shop in the whole town which sold this miraculous drug, and that was nearly two miles from our house. However, this was not like the case of the ardisia which we groped in the dark to find. After making out his prescription Dr. Chen Lianhe gave me earnest and detailed instructions as to where to obtain it.

'I have one medicine', Dr. Chen told my father once, 'which applied to the tongue would do you good, I'm sure. For the tongue is the intelligent sprout of the heart. . . . It is not expensive either, only two dollars a box. . . .'

My father thought for some time, then shook his head.

'This present treatment may not prove too effective,' said Dr. Chen another day. 'I think we might ask a diviner if there is not some avenging spirit behind this. . . . A doctor can cure diseases but not fate, isn't that correct? Of course, this may be something that happened in a previous existence. . . .'

---

[1] 洋 meaning 'foreign' contains 羊 meaning 'sheep', and both words are pronounced 'yang'.

My father thought for some time, then shook his head.

All the best doctors can bring the dead to life, as we know from the placards to this effect which we see when we walk past their doors. But now a concession has been made, for physicians themselves admit: 'Western doctors are best at surgery, while Chinese doctors are best at internal medicine.' But there was no Western-trained doctor in S—— at that time. Indeed it had never occurred to anyone that there was such a thing in the world as a Western doctor. Hence, whenever anyone fell ill, all we could do was ask the direct descendants of the Yellow Emperor and Chi Po [1] to cure him. In the days of the Yellow Emperor, wizards and doctors were one; thus right down to the present his disciples can still see ghosts and believe that 'the tongue is the intelligent sprout of the heart'. This is the 'fate' of Chinese, which not even famous physicians are able to cure.

When he would not apply the efficacious remedy on his tongue and could not think of any avenging spirit he had wronged, naturally it was no use my father simply eating broken-drum boluses for over a hundred days. These drum pills proved unable to beat the dropsy, and finally my father lay at his last gasp on his bed. We invited Dr. Chen Lianhe once more—an emergency call this time, for ten silver dollars. Once more, he calmly wrote out a prescription. He discontinued the broken-drum boluses, however, and the adjuvant was not too mysterious either; so before very long this medicine was ready. But when we poured it between my father's lips, it trickled out again from one side of his mouth.

That ended my dealings with Dr. Chen Lianhe; but I sometimes saw him in the street being carried swiftly by in his fast sedan chair with three carriers. I hear he is still in good health, practising medicine and editing a paper on traditional Chinese medicine, engaging in a struggle with those Western-trained doctors who are good for nothing but surgery.

There is indeed a slight difference between the Chinese and Western outlook. I understand that when a filial son in China knows that his parents' end is approaching, he buys several catties of ginseng, boils it, and gives it to them, in the hope of

[1] Legendary figures regarded as the inventors of medicine, to whom the earliest medical books in China are attributed.

prolonging their lives a few more days or even half a day. One of my professors, whose subject was medicine, told me that a doctor's duty was to cure those who could be cured, and see to it that those who could not died without suffering. But this professor, of course, was Western-trained.

Father's breathing became very laboured, until even I could scarcely bear to hear it; but nobody could help him. Sometimes the thought flashed into my mind, 'Better if it could all be over quickly. . . .' At once I knew I should not think of such a thing, in fact it was wicked. But at the same time I felt this idea was only proper, for I loved my father dearly. Even today, I still feel the same about it.

That morning Mrs. Yan, who lived in the same compound, came in. An authority on etiquette, she told us not to wait there doing nothing. So we changed his clothes, burnt paper coins and something called the *Gaowang Sutra*,[1] and put the ashes, wrapped in paper, in his hand. . . .

'Call him!' said Mrs. Yan. 'Your father's at his last gasp. Call him quickly!'

'Father! Father!' I called accordingly.

'Louder. He can't hear. Hurry up, can't you?'

'Father! Father!!'

His face, which had been composed, grew suddenly tense again; and he raised his eyelids slightly, as if in pain.

'Call him!' she insisted. 'Hurry up and call him!'

'Father!!!'

'What is it? . . . Don't shout. . . . Don't . . .'

His voice was low, and once more he started panting for breath. It was some time before he recovered his earlier calm.

'Father!!!'

I went on calling until he breathed his last.

I can still hear my voice as it sounded then. And each time I hear those cries, I feel this was the greatest wrong I ever did my father.

7 October 1926

---

[1] It was believed that by burning this sutra you could lessen the torments of a man in hell. Paper coins were burnt so that the dead man would have money to spend.

Poems and Prose Poems

A Lament for Fan Ainong[1]

哀范君三章

In a time of wind and storm
I mourn for Fan Ainong,
My friend with grey and thinning hair
Who scorned the grubbing insects.
This world turns bitter as wormwood—
Where is a place for honest men?
Three short months ago we parted
And now this eccentric is gone.

The grass on China's coast grew green
Long as you lingered in a foreign land;
As the foxes fled their den
Peach-wood puppets took the stage;
Bleak clouds hung over our home,
Even sultry nights dragged chill and long;
Alone you sank beneath the clear cold waves—
Did they wash your troubled heart?

How often we discussed our times over wine
(You who looked down on drinking!)
In a world blind drunk
A mere tippler might well drown;
Our last farewell has parted us for ever,
Your thought-provoking words are at an end;
Like scattering clouds my friend has gone,
And I am but a grain of dust in the wind.

1912

[1] Like Lu Xun, Fan Ainong came from Shaoxing and studied in Japan. In 1911, when Lu Xun became principal of Shaoxing Normal School, he appointed Fan as dean of studies. Dismissed by Lu Xun's successor, Fan went through hard times. In 1912, on his way back by boat from seeing an opera, he fell into the river and was drowned. Because he was a good swimmer, Lu Xun suspected that he had committed suicide.

Revenge 复　仇　（其二）

Because he thinks himself the son of God, the king of the Jews, he is to be crucified.

The soldiers put on him a purple robe, make him wear a crown of thorns, and wish him joy. Then they beat his head with a reed, spit upon him, and bow the knee before him. After they have mocked him, they strip off his purple robe and leave him wearing his own clothes as before.

See how they beat his head, spit upon him, kneel before him. . . .

He will not drink the wine mixed with myrrh, for he wants to remain sober to savour the Israelites' treatment of their Son of God, and have longer to pity their future but hate their present.

All around is hate, pitiable, execrable.

Hammering is heard, and nails pierce his palms. But the fact that these pitiable creatures are crucifying their Son of God makes him feel less pain. Hammering is heard and nails pierce the soles of his feet, breaking a bone so that pain shoots through his marrow. But the fact that these execrable creatures are crucifying their Son of God comforts him in his pain.

The cross is hoisted up. He is hanging in mid-air.

He has not drunk the wine mixed with myrrh. He wants to remain sober to savour the Israelites' treatment of their Son of God, and to have longer to pity their future but hate their present.

All the passers-by insult and curse him, the chief priests and the scribes also mock him, the two thieves being crucified with him laugh at him too.

Even those being crucified with him . . .

All around is hate, pitiable, execrable.

In the pain from his hands and feet he savours the sorrow of the pitiable creatures who are crucifying

the Son of God, and the joy of the execrable creatures
who are crucifying the Son of God and who know
that the Son of God is about to die. Sudden agony
from his broken bones shoots to his heart and
marrow, intoxicating him with great ecstasy and
compassion.

His belly heaves in the agony of compassion and
execration.

There is darkness over all the earth.

'*Eli, Eli, lama sabachthani*?' (My God, my God,
why hast thou forsaken me?)

God has forsaken him, and so he is the son of man
after all. But the Israelites are crucifying even the
son of man.

Those who reek most of blood and filth are not
those who crucify the Son of God, but those who
crucify the son of man.

20 December 1924

Hope   希　　望

My heart is extraordinarily lonely.

But my heart is very tranquil, void of love and
hate, joy and sadness, colour and sound.

I am probably growing old. Is it not a fact that my
hair is turning white? Is it not a fact that my hands
are trembling? Then the hands of my spirit must also
be trembling. The hair of my spirit must also be
turning white.

But this has been the case for many years.

Before that my heart once overflowed with san-
guinary songs, blood and iron, fire and poison,
resurgence and revenge. Then suddenly my heart
became empty, except when I sometimes deliber-

121

ately filled it with vain, self-deluding hope. Hope, hope—I took this shield of hope to withstand the invasion of the dark night in the emptiness, although behind this shield there was still dark night and emptiness. But even so I slowly wasted my youth.

I knew, of course, that my youth had perished. But I thought that the youth outside still existed: stars and moonlight, dead fallen butterflies, flowers in the darkness, the ill-omened call of the owl, the weeping with blood of the nightingale, the indecision of laughter, the dance of love. . . . Although it might be a youth of sadness and uncertainty, it was still youth.

But why is it now so lonely? Is it because even the youth outside me has perished, and the young people of the world have all grown old?

I have to grapple alone with the dark night in the emptiness. I put down the shield of hope, hearing the *Song of Hope* by Sándor Petöfi:

> What is Hope? A prostitute!
> Alluring to all, she gives herself to all,
> Until you have sacrificed a priceless treasure—
> Your youth—then she forsakes you.

It is already seventy-five years since this great lyric poet and Hungarian patriot died for his fatherland on the spears of the Cossacks. However tragic his death, it is even sadder that his poetry has not yet died.

But—so wretched is life—even a man as daring and resolute as Petöfi had in the end to halt before the dark night and gaze back towards the distant Orient.

'Despair, like hope,' he said, 'is but vanity.'

If I must still live in this vanity which is neither light nor darkness, then I would seek the youth of sadness and uncertainty which has perished, even though it is outside me. For once the youth outside me vanishes, my own old age will also wither away.

But now there are neither stars nor moonlight, no

dead fallen butterflies, no indecision of laughter, no dance of love. The young people are very placid.

So I have to grapple alone with the dark night in the emptiness. Even if I cannot find the youth outside me, I would at least cast aside my own old age. But where is the dark night? Now there are neither stars nor moonlight, no indecision of laughter, no dance of love. The young people of the world are very placid, and before me there is not even a real dark night.

Despair, like hope, is but vanity.

New Year's Day 1925

The Dog's Retort   狗 的 驳 诘

I dreamed I was walking in a narrow lane, my clothes in rags, like a beggar.

A dog started barking behind me.

I looked back contemptuously and shouted at him:

'Bah! Shut up! You fawn on the rich and bully the poor!'

He sniggered.

'So sorry,' he said, 'we are not as good as men.'

'What!' Quite outraged, I felt that this was the supreme insult.

'I'm ashamed to say I still don't know how to distinguish between copper and silver, between silk and cloth, between officials and common citizens, between masters and their slaves, between . . .'

I turned and fled.

'Wait a bit! Let us talk some more. . . .' From behind he urged me loudly to stay.

But I ran straight on as fast as I could, until I

123

had run right out of my dream and was back in my own bed.

23 April 1925

The Good Hell that was Lost

失 掉 的 好 地 獄

I dreamed I was lying in bed in the wilderness beside hell. The deep yet orderly wailing of all the ghosts blended with the roar of flames, the seething of oil and the clashing of iron prongs to make one vast intoxicating harmony, proclaiming to all three worlds the peace of the lower realm.

Before me stood a great man, beautiful and benign, his whole body radiant with light; but I knew he was the Devil.

'This is the end of everything! The end of everything! The wretched ghosts have lost their good hell.'

He spoke with indignation, then sat down to tell me a story that he knew.

'It was when heaven and earth were made honey-coloured that the Devil overcame God and wielded absolute power. He held heaven, earth, and hell. Then he came in person to hell and sat in the midst of it, radiating bright light over all the ghosts.

'Hell had long been neglected: the spiked trees had lost their glitter, the verge of the boiling oil no longer seethed, at times the great fires merely gave off a little grey smoke, and far off there even bloomed some mandrake flowers, though their blossoms were very small, pale, and wretched. But that was not to be wondered at, for the earth had been fearfully burnt and had naturally lost its fertility.

'Awaking amid the cold oil and lukewarm fires, by the light of the Devil the ghosts saw the little flowers of hell, so pale and wretched, and were completely bewitched. They suddenly remembered the world of men, and after reflecting for none knows how many years they sent up towards mankind a great cry denouncing hell.

'Man responded and arose; upholding the right he fought against the Devil. Louder than thunder, the tumult of fighting filled all three worlds. At last, by dint of great guile and cunning snares, he forced the Devil to withdraw from hell. After the final victory, the flag of mankind was hoisted over the gate of hell.

'The ghosts were still rejoicing together when man's commissioner to reorganize hell arrived. Invested with the majesty of man, he sat down in the middle of hell and ruled over the ghosts.

'When the ghosts uttered another desperate howl against hell, they became rebels against man. Condemned to eternal damnation for this crime, they were banished to the midst of the spiked trees.

'Man then wielded absolute power over hell, his authority exceeding that of the Devil. He reconstructed the ruins, having given the highest post to the Ox-Headed One. He also added fuel to the fires, sharpened the sword-hills, and changed the whole face of hell, doing away with the former decadence.

'At once the mandrake flowers withered. The oil seethed as before, the swords were sharp as before, the fires blazed as before, and the ghosts groaned and writhed as before, until none of them had time to regret the good hell that was lost.

'This was man's success, the Devil's misfortune. . .

'Friend, I see you mistrust me. Yes, you are a man. I must go to look for wild beasts and ghosts. . . .'

16 June 1925

125

On Expressing an Opinion 立 论

I dreamed I was in the classroom of a primary school preparing to write an essay, and asked the teacher how to express an opinion.

'That's hard!' Glancing sideways at me over his glasses he said: 'Let me tell you a story—

'When a son is born to a family, the whole household is delighted. When he is one month old they carry him out to display him to the guests—usually expecting some compliments, of course.

'One says: "This child will be rich." He is heartily thanked.

'One says: "This child will be an official." Some compliments are paid him in return.

'One says: "This child will die." He is thoroughly beaten by the whole family.

'That the child will die is inevitable, while to say that he will be rich or a high official may be a lie. Yet the lie is rewarded, whereas the statement of the inevitable gains a beating. You . . .'

'I don't want to tell lies, sir, neither do I want to be beaten. So what should I say?'

'In that case, say: "Aha! Just look at this child! My word . . . Did you ever! Oho! Hehe! He, hehehehe!"'

8 July 1925

Such a Fighter 这 样 的 战 士

There will be such a fighter!

No longer ignorant as the African natives shouldering well-polished Mausers, nor listless as the Chinese green-banner troops[1] carrying light machine-guns. He does not rely on armour made of ox-hide or of scrap-iron. He has nothing but himself, and for weapon nothing but the javelin hurled by barbarians.

He walks into the lines of nothingness, where all who meet him nod to him in the same manner. He knows that this nod is a weapon used by the enemy to kill without bloodshed, by which many fighters have perished. Like a cannon-ball, it renders ineffective the strength of the brave.

Above their heads hang all sorts of flags and banners, embroidered with all manner of titles: philanthropist, scholar, writer, elder, youth, dilettante, gentleman . . . Beneath are all sorts of surcoats, embroidered with all manner of fine names: scholarship, morality, national culture, public opinion, logic, justice, Asian civilization. . . .

But he raises his javelin.

Together they give their solemn oath that their hearts are in the centre of their chests, as is not the case with other prejudiced people. They hope to prove by their breast-plates that they themselves believe their hearts are in the centre of their chests.

But he raises his javelin.

He smiles and hurls his javelin off-centre, and it pierces them through the heart.

All crumble and fall to the ground, leaving only a surcoat in which there is nothing. The nothingness

[1] The Qing dynasty army was divided into eight 'banners'. The green-banner troops were Han (chinese) soldiers who had gone over to the Manchus.

has escaped and won the victory, because now it has become the criminal who killed the philanthropist and the rest.

But he raises his javelin.

He walks with great strides through the ranks of nothingness, and sees again the same nods, the same banners and surcoats. . . .

But he raises his javelin.

At last he grows old and dies of old age in the lines of nothingness. He is not a fighter after all, and the nothingness is the victor.

In such a place no tumult of fighting is heard, but there is peace.

Peace . . .

But he raises his javelin!

14 December 1925

The Wise Man, the Fool, and the Slave

聪 明 人 和 傻 子 和 奴 才

A slave did nothing but look for people to whom to pour out his woes. This was all he would and all he could do. One day he met a wise man.

'Sir!' he cried sadly, tears streaming from his eyes. 'You know, the life I lead is less than human. I may not have a single meal all day, and if I do it is only husks of sorghum which not even a pig or dog would eat. Not to mention that there is only one small bowl of it. . . .'

'That's really pitiful,' the wise man commiserated.

'Isn't it?' His spirits rose. 'Then I work all day and all night. At dawn I carry water, at dusk I cook the dinner; in the morning I run errands, in the evening I grind wheat; when it's fine I wash the clothes, when it's wet I hold the umbrella; in winter I mind the boiler, in summer I wave the fan. At midnight I boil mushrooms, and wait on our master at his gambling parties; but never a tip do I get, only sometimes the strap. . . .'

'Dear me . . .' The wise man sighed, and the rims of his eyes looked a little red as if he were going to shed tears.

'I can't go on like this, sir. I must find some way out. But what can I do?'

'I am sure things will improve. . . .'

'Do you think so? I certainly hope so. But now that I've told you my troubles and you've been so sympathetic and encouraging, I already feel much better. It shows there is still some justice in the world.'

A few days later, though, he felt aggrieved again and found someone else to whom to pour out his woes.

'Sir!' he exclaimed, shedding tears. 'You know, where I live is even worse than a pigsty. My master doesn't treat me like a human being; he treats his dog ten thousand times better. . . .'

'Confound him!' The other swore so loudly that he startled the slave. The other man was a fool.

'All I have to live in, sir, is a tumble-down one-roomed hut, damp, cold, and swarming with bed-bugs. They bite me like anything when I lie down to sleep. The place stinks and hasn't a single window. . . .'

'Can't you ask your master to have a window made?'

'How can I do that?'

'Well, show me what it's like.'

The fool followed the slave to his hut, and began to pound the mud wall.

'What are you doing, sir?' The slave was horrified.

'I am opening a window for you.'

'This won't do! The master will curse me.'

'Let him!' The fool continued to pound away.

'Help! A bandit is breaking down the house! Come

quickly or he will knock down the wall!' Shouting and sobbing, the slave rolled frantically on the ground. A whole troop of slaves came out and drove away the fool. Roused by the outcry, the last one to come slowly out was the master.

'A bandit tried to break down our house. I gave the alarm, and together we drove him away!' The slave spoke respectfully and triumphantly.

'Good for you!' The master praised him.

Many callers came that day to express concern, among them the wise man.

'Sir, because I made myself useful, the master praised me. When you said the other day that things would improve, you were really showing foresight.' He spoke very hopefully and happily.

'That's right. . . .' replied the wise man, and seemed happy for his sake.

26 December 1925

Amid Pale Bloodstains

淡 淡 的 血 痕 中

> In memory of some who are dead, some who live, and some yet unborn.

At present the creator is still a weakling.

In secret, he causes heaven and earth to change, but dares not destroy this world. In secret, he causes living creatures to die, but dares not preserve their dead bodies. In secret, he causes mankind to shed blood, but dares not keep the bloodstains fresh for ever. In secret, he causes mankind to suffer pain, but dares not let them remember it for ever.

He provides for his kind only, the weaklings among men; using deserted ruins and lonely tombs to set

130

off rich mansions; using time to dilute pain and bloodstains; each day pouring out one cup of slightly sweetened bitter wine—neither too little nor too much—to cause slight intoxication. This he gives to mankind so that those who drink it weep and sing, are both sober and drunk, conscious and unconscious, eager to live and eager to die. He must make all creatures wish to live on. He has not the courage yet to destroy mankind.

A few deserted ruins and a few lonely tombs are scattered over the earth, reflected by pale bloodstains; and there men taste their own vague pain and sorrow, as well as that of others. They will not spurn it, however, thinking it better than nothing; and they call themselves 'victims of heaven' to justify their tasting this pain and sorrow. In apprehensive silence they await the coming of new pain and sorrow, new suffering which appals them, which they none the less thirst to meet.

All these are the loyal subjects of the creator. This is what he wants them to be.

A rebellious fighter has arisen from mankind, who, standing erect, sees through all the deserted ruins and lonely tombs of the past and the present. He remembers all the intense and unending agony; he gazes at the whole mass of congealed blood; he understands all that is dead and all that is living, as well as all yet unborn. He sees through the creator's game. And he will arise to save or destroy mankind, these loyal subjects of the creator.

The creator, the weakling, hides himself in shame. Then heaven and earth change colour in the eyes of the fighter.

8 April 1926

Long Nights   惯 于 长 夜

Used to the long nights of springtime,
My hair grows white as I hide with my wife and son;
Dreams show my dear mother in tears
And the chieftains' flags over the city are always changing.
Cruel to see my friends become fresh ghosts!
Raging I turn on the bayonets and write these lines.
Will they ever see print? I frown,
While moonlight glimmers like liquid on my dark gown.

1931

A Lament for Yang Quan[1]   悼 杨 铨

My fire of days gone by has cooled;
What matter if flowers bloom or fade?
I did not think in the tears of the southern rain
To weep again for this fine son of China.

1933

[1] On 18 June 1933 Yang Quan, a progressive intellectual and prominent member of the China League for Civil Rights, was murdered by Kuomintang agents. On 20 June, a rainy day, Lu Xun went at considerable personal risk to attend his funeral.

A Poem　　　　　　　无　　题

A host of dark, gaunt faces in the brambles,
Yet who dare shake the earth with lamentation?
I brood over our whole far-stretching land
And in this silence hear the peal of thunder.[1]

1934

Written in Late Autumn　　亥 年 残 秋 偶 作

Dismayed by a world in the grip of autumn,
How is my brush to be dipped in the warmth of spring?
Passions drowned in this grey ocean of dust,
Wind chilling the officials departing their posts.
Returning, old, to a marsh naked of reeds,
I fall in dream through clouds that freeze my veins;
Waiting for cockcrow I hear only the night's silence,
Rising I see the Dipper low in the sky.

1935

[1] An allusion to the rising storm of revolution.

Essays

My Views on Chastity　　我 的 节 烈 观

'The world is going to the dogs. Men are growing more degenerate every day. The country is faced with ruin!'—such laments have been heard in China since time immemorial. But 'degeneracy' varies from age to age. It used to mean one thing, now it means another. Except in memorials to the throne and the like, in which no one dares make wild statements, this is the tone of all written and spoken pronouncements. For not only is such carping good for people; it removes the speaker from the ranks of the degenerate. That gentlemen sigh when they meet is only natural. But now even murderers, incendiaries, libertines, swindlers, and other scoundrels shake their heads in the intervals between their crimes and mutter: 'Men are growing more degenerate every day!'

As far as morality goes, inciters to evil are not the only degenerates. So are those who simply condone it, delight in it, or deplore it. That is why some men this year have actually not contented themselves with empty talk, but after expressing their horror have looked around for a remedy. The first was Kang Youwei.[1] Stamping and sawing the air, he declared 'constitutional monarchy' the panacea. He was refuted by Chen Duxiu,[2] who was followed by the spiritualists who somehow or other hit on the weird idea of inviting the ghost of Mencius to devise a policy for them. However, Chen Bainian, Qian Xuantong, and Liu Bannong[3] swear they are talking nonsense.

[1] Kang Youwei (1858–1927), who led the 1898 reform movement, in 1918 published an article declaring that China was not yet ripe for democracy.

[2] Chen Duxiu (1880–1942), then chief editor of the magazine *New Youth*, published an article there refuting Kang Youwei's ideas.

[3] In 1918 *New Youth* carried articles by these three professors at Peking University inveighing against the spiritualist school and advocating a return to the past.

Those articles refuting them in *New Youth* are enough to make one's blood run cold. This is the twentieth century, and dawn has already broken on mankind. If *New Youth* were to carry an article debating whether the earth were square or round, readers would almost certainly sit up. Yet their present arguments are pretty well on a par with contending that the earth is not square. That such a debate should continue *today* is enough to make anyone's blood run cold!

Though constitutional monarchy is no longer discussed, the spiritualists still seem to be going strong. But they have failed to satisfy another group, who continue to shake their heads and mutter: 'Men are growing more degenerate every day.' These, in fact, have thought up a different remedy, which they call 'extolling chastity'.

For many years now, ever since the failure of the reformists and the call for a return to the past, devices like this have been generally approved: all we are now doing is raising the old banners. Moreover, in step with this, writers and public speakers keep singing the praises of chastity. This is their only way to rise above those who are 'growing more degenerate every day'.

Chastity used to be a virtue for men as well as women, hence the references to 'chaste gentlemen' in our literature. However, the chastity which is extolled today is for women only—men have no part in it. According to contemporary moralists, a chaste woman is one who does not remarry or run off with a lover after her husband's death, while the earlier her husband dies and the poorer her family the more chaste it is possible for her to be. In addition, there are two other types of chaste woman: one kills herself when her husband or fiancé dies; the other manages to commit suicide when confronted by a ravisher, or meets her death while resisting. The more cruel her death, the greater glory she wins. If she is surprised and ravished but kills herself afterwards, there is bound to be talk. She has one chance in ten thousand of finding a generous moralist who may excuse her in view of the circumstances and grant her the title 'chaste'. But no man of letters will want to write her biography and, if forced to, he is sure to end on a note of disapproval.

In short, when a woman's husband dies she should remain single or die. If she meets a ravisher she should also die. When such women are praised, it shows that society is morally sound and there is still hope for China. That is the gist of the matter.

Kang Youwei had to use the emperor's name; the spiritualists depend on superstitious nonsense; but upholding chastity is entirely up to the people. This shows we are coming on. However, there are still some questions I would like to raise, which I shall try to answer according to my own lights. Moreover, since I take it that this idea of saving the world through chastity is held by the majority of my countrymen, those who expound it being merely their spokesmen who voice something which affects the whole body corporate, I am putting my questions and answers before the majority of the people.

My first question is: In what way do unchaste women injure the country? It is only too clear today that 'the country is faced with ruin'. There is no end to the dastardly crimes committed and war, banditry, famine, flood, and drought follow one after the other. But this is owing to the fact that we have no new morality or new science and all our thoughts and actions are out of date. That is why these benighted times resemble the old dark ages. Besides, all government, army, academic, and business posts are filled by men, not by unchaste women. And it can hardly be because the men in power have been bewitched by such women that they lose all sense of right and wrong and plunge into dissipation. As for flood, drought, and famine, they result from a lack of modern knowledge, from worshipping dragons and snakes, cutting down forests, and neglecting water conservancy—they have even less to do with women. War and banditry, it is true, often produce a crop of unchaste women; but the war and banditry come first, and the unchaste women follow. It is not women's wantonness that causes such troubles.

My second question is: Why should women shoulder the whole responsibility for saving the world? According to the old school, women belong to the *yin*[1] or negative element. Their place is in the home, as chattels of men. Surely, then, the onus for governing the state and saving the country should rest with

[1] Certain Confucians claimed that all phenomena resulted from the interaction of the positive principle *yang* and the negative principle *yin*.

the men, who belong to the *yang* or positive element. How can we burden weak females with such a tremendous task? And according to the moderns, both sexes are equal with roughly the same obligations. Though women have their duties, they should not have more than their share. It is up to the men to play their part as well, not just by combating violence but by exercising their own masculine virtues. It is not enough merely to punish and lecture the women.

My third question is: What purpose is served by upholding chastity? If we grade all the women in the world according to their chastity, we shall probably find that they fall into three classes: those who are chaste and should be praised; those who are unchaste; and those who have not yet married or whose husbands are still alive, who have not yet met a ravisher, and whose chastity therefore cannot yet be gauged. The first class is doing very nicely with all these encomiums, so we can pass over it. And the second class is beyond hope, for there has never been any room for repentance in China once a woman has erred—she can only die of shame. This is not worth dwelling on either. The third class, therefore, is the most important. Now that their hearts have been touched, they must have vowed to themselves: 'If my husband dies, I shall never marry again. If I meet a ravisher, I shall kill myself as fast as ever I can.' But what effect, pray, do such decisions have upon public morality which, as pointed out earlier, is determined by men?

And here another question arises. These chaste women who have been praised are naturally paragons of virtue. But though all may aspire to be saints, not all can be models of chastity. Some of the women in the third class may have the noblest resolutions, but what if their husbands live to a ripe old age and the world remains at peace? They will just have to suffer in silence, doomed to be second-class citizens all their lives.

So far we have simply used old-world common sense, yet even so we have found much that is contradictory. If we live at all in the twentieth century, two more points will occur to us.

First of all: Is chastity a virtue? Virtues should be universal, required of all, within the reach of all, and beneficial to others as well as oneself. Only then are they worth having. But in addition to the fact that all men are excluded from what goes by the name of chastity today, not even all women are eligible for this honour. Hence it cannot be counted a virtue, or held up as an example. . . . When a rough man swoops down on one of the weaker sex (women are still weak as things stand today), if her father, brothers, and husband cannot save her and the neighbours fail her too, her best course is to die. She may, of course, die after being defiled; or she may not die at all. Later on, her father, brothers, husband, and neighbours will get together with the writers, scholars, and moralists; and, no whit abashed by their own cowardice and incompetence, nor concerned how to punish the criminal, will start wagging their tongues. Is she dead or not? Was she raped or not? How gratifying if she has died, how shocking if she has not! So they create all these glorious women martyrs on the one hand and these wantons universally condemned on the other. If we think this over soberly, we can see that, far from being praiseworthy, it is absolutely inhuman.

Our second query is: Have polygamous men the right to praise chastity in women? The old moralists would say, of course they have: the mere fact that they are men makes them different from other people and sole arbiters of society. Relying on the ancient concept of *yin* and *yang* or the negative and the positive, they like to show off to women. But people today have had a glimpse of the truth and know that this talk of *yin* and *yang* is absolute gibberish. Even if there are dual principles, there is no way of proving that *yang* is nobler than *yin*, the male superior to the female. Besides, society and the state are not built by men only. Hence we must accept the truth that the two sexes are equal. And if equal they should be bound by the same contract. Men cannot make rules for women which they do not keep themselves. Moreover, if marriage is a sale, swindle, or form of tribute, a husband has no right even to demand that his wife remain faithful to him during his lifetime. How can he, a polygamist, praise a woman for following her husband to the grave?

This ends my questions and answers. The moralists' case is so weak it is strange it should have survived to the present time.

To understand this, we must see how this thing called chastity originated and spread, and why it has remained unchanged.

In ancient society women were usually the chattels of men, who could kill them, eat them, or do what they pleased with them. After a man's death, there was naturally no objection to burying his women with his favourite treasures or weapons. By degrees, however, this practice of burying women alive stopped and the conception of chastity came into being. But it was mainly because a widow was the wife of a dead man whose ghost was following her that other men dared not marry her—not because it was thought wrong for a woman to marry twice. This is still the case in primitive societies today. We have no means of ascertaining what happened in China in remote antiquity; but by the end of the Zhou dynasty (1066–771 B.C.) the retainers buried with their masters included men as well as women, and widows were free to marry again. It appears then that this custom died out very early. From the Han (206 B.C.–220 A.D.) to the Tang dynasty (618–907) no one advocated chastity. It was only in the Song dynasty (960–1279) that professional Confucians[1] started saying: 'Starving to death is a small matter, but losing one's chastity is a great calamity.' And they would exclaim in horror when they read of some woman in history who married twice. Whether they were sincere or not we shall never know. That was when men were beginning to grow 'more degenerate every day', the country was 'faced with ruin', and the people were in a bad way; so it is possible that these professional Confucians were using women's chastity to lash the men. But since this type of insinuation is rather contemptible and its aim was far from clear, though it may have resulted in a slight increase in the number of chaste women, men in general remained unmoved. And so China, with 'the oldest civilization in the world and the highest moral standard', 'by the grace of God and the will of Heaven' fell into the hands of Sechen Khan, Öljäitü Khan, Kuluk Khan,[2] and all the rest of them. After several more changes of rulers, the conception of chastity developed further. The more loyalty the emperor

[1] The neo-Confucians of the Song dynasty, self-styled champions of morality.

[2] All the emperors during the Yuan dynasty (1279–1368) had Mongolian titles. Sechen Khan is better known by his personal name Khubilai.

demanded of his subjects, the more chastity the men required of the women. By the Qing dynasty (1644–1911) Confucian scholars had grown even stricter. When they read in a Tang dynasty history of a princess who married again, they would thunder in great indignation: 'What is this! How dare the man cast such aspersions on royalty!' Had that Tang historian been alive at the time, he would certainly have been struck off the official list, to 'rectify men's hearts and mend their morals'.

So when the country is about to be conquered, there is much talk of chastity and women who take their own lives are highly regarded. For women belong to men, and when a man dies his wife should not remarry; much less should she be snatched from him during his life. But since he himself is one of a conquered people, with no power to protect his wife and no courage to resist, he finds a way out by urging her to kill herself. There are rich men, too, with whole bevies of wives, daughters, concubines, and maids, who cannot look after them all during times of trouble. Confronted by rebels or government troops, they are absolutely helpless. All they can do is to save their own skin and urge their women to seek a glorious death, for then they will be of no interest to the rebels. Then when order is restored, these rich men can saunter back to utter a few encomiums over the dead. For a man to remarry is quite in order anyway, so they get some other women and that is that. This is why we find works like *The Death of Two Virtuous Widows* or *The Seven Concubines' Epitaph*. Even the writings of Qian Qianyi[1] are filled with accounts of chaste women and praise of their glorious death.

Only a society where each cares solely for himself and women must remain chaste while men are polygamous, could create such a perverted morality, which becomes more exacting and cruel with each passing day. There is nothing strange about this. But since man proposes and woman suffers, why is it women have never uttered a protest? Because submission is the cardinal wifely virtue. Of course a woman needs no education: even to open her mouth is counted a crime. Since her spirit is

[1] (1582–1664). Minister of Ceremony at the end of the Ming dynasty, he was a traitor who welcomed in the Manchu invaders.

as distorted as her body,[1] she has no objection to this distorted morality. And even a woman with views of her own has no chance to express them. If she writes a few poems on moonlight and flowers, men may accuse her of looking for a lover. Then how dare she challenge this 'eternal truth'? Some stories, indeed, tell of women who for various reasons would not remain chaste. But the story-tellers always point out that a widow who remarries is either caught by her first husband's ghost and carried off to hell or, condemned by the whole world, becomes a beggar who is turned away from every door till she dies a wretched death.

This being the case, women had no choice but to submit. But why did the men let it go at that? The fact is that after the Han dynasty most mediums of public opinion were in the hands of professional Confucians, much more so from the Song and Yuan dynasties onwards. There is hardly a single book not written by these orthodox scholars. They are the only ones to express opinions. With the exception of Buddhists and Taoists who were permitted by imperial decree to voice their opinions, no other 'heresies' could take a single step into the open. Moreover, most men were very much influenced by the Confucians' self-vaunted 'tractability'. To do anything unorthodox was taboo. So even those who realized the truth were not prepared to give up their lives for it. Everyone knew that a woman could lose her chastity only through a man. Still they went on blaming the woman alone, while the man who destroyed a widow's reputation by marrying her or the ruffian who forced her to die unchaste was passed over in silence. Men, after all, are more formidable than women, and to bring someone to justice is harder than to utter praise. A few men with some sense of fair play, it is true, suggested mildly that it was unnecessary for girls to follow their betrothed into the grave; but the world did not listen to them. Had they persisted, they would have been thought intolerable and treated like unchaste women; so they turned 'tractable' and held their peace. This is why there has been no change right up till now.

(I should mention here, however, that among the present champions of chastity are quite a few people whom I know. I

[1] This refers to the practice of binding women's feet.

am sure there are good men among them, men with the best
intentions, but their way of saving society is wrong. To go
north they have headed west. And we cannot expect them,
just because they are good, to be able to end up north by going
due west. So I hope they will turn back.)

Then there is another question.

Is it difficult to be chaste? The answer is, very. It is because
men know how difficult it is that they praise it. Public opinion
has always taken it for granted that chastity depends upon the
woman. Though a man may seduce a woman, he is not brought
to book. If A (a man) makes advances to B (a woman) but she
rejects him, then she is chaste. If she dies in the process, she is
a glorious martyr: A's name is unsullied and society undefiled.
If, on the other hand, B accepts A, she is unchaste; again A's
name is unsullied, but she has lowered the tone of society. This
happens in other cases too. A country's downfall, for instance, is
always blamed on women. Willy-nilly they have shouldered
the sins of mankind for more than three thousand years. Since
men are not brought to book and have no sense of shame, they
go on seducing women just as they please, while writers treat
such incidents as romantic. Thus a woman is beset by danger
on every side. With the exception of her father, brothers, and
husband, all men are potential seducers. That is why I say it is
difficult to be chaste.

Is it painful to be chaste? The answer is, very. It is because
men know how painful it is that they praise it. Everyone wants
to live, yet to become a martyr means certain death—this needs
no explanation. A chaste widow, however, lives on. We can
take her grief for granted, but her physical existence is also a
hard one. If women had independent means and people helped
each other, a widow could manage on her own; but unfortunately the reverse is the case in China. So if she has money she is
all right, if she is poor she can only starve to death. And not
till she has starved to death will she be honoured and her name
recorded in the local history. Invariably the records of different
districts contain a few sections headed 'Women Martyrs', a line
or half a line for each. They may be called Zhao, Qian, Sun, or
Li, but who cares to read about them? Even the great moralists
who have worshipped chastity all their lives may not be able

to tell you offhand the names of the first ten martyrs of their
honourable district; so alive or dead such women are cut off
from the rest of the world. That is why I say it is painful to be
chaste.

In that case, is it less painful not to be chaste? No, that is very
painful too. Since the public looks down on such women, they
are social outcasts. Many of the tenets carelessly handed down
by the ancients are completely irrational, yet the weight of
tradition and numbers can crush undesirable characters to
death. God knows how many murders these anonymous,
unconscious assassins have committed since ancient times,
including the murder of chaste women. They are honoured
after their death, though, by mention in the local histories,
while unchaste women are abused by everyone during their
lifetime and suffer meaningless persecution. That is why I say
their lot is also very painful.

Are women themselves in favour of chastity? The answer is:
No, they are not. All human beings have their ideals and hopes.
Whether high or low, their life must have a meaning. What
benefits others as well as oneself is best, but at least we expect to
benefit ourselves. To be chaste is difficult and painful, of profit
neither to others nor to oneself; so to say that women are in
favour of it is really unreasonable. Hence if you meet any
young woman and in all sincerity beg her to become a martyr,
she will fly into a passion, and you may even receive a blow from
the respected fist of her father, brothers, or husband. Nevertheless this practice persists, supported as it is by tradition and
numbers. Yet there is no one but fears this thing 'chastity'.
Women fear to be crucified by it, while men fear for their near-
est and dearest. That is why I say no one is in favour of it.

On the basis of the facts and reasons stated above, I affirm
that to be chaste is exceedingly difficult and painful, favoured
by no one, of profit neither to others nor oneself, of no service
to the state or society, and of no value at all to posterity. It has
lost any vigour it had and all reason for existing.

Finally I have one last question.

If chastity has lost any vigour it had and all reason for
existing, are the sufferings of chaste women completely in vain?

My answer is: They still deserve compassion. These women

are to be pitied. Trapped for no good reason by tradition and numbers, they are sacrificed to no purpose. We should hold a great memorial service to them.

After mourning for the dead, we must swear to be more intelligent, brave, aspiring, and progressive. We must tear off every mask. We must do away with all the stupidity and tyranny in the world which injure others as well as ourselves.

After mourning for the dead, we must swear to get rid of the meaningless suffering which blights our lives. We must do away with all the stupidity and tyranny which create and relish the sufferings of others.

We must also swear to see to it that all mankind know true happiness.

July 1918

What Happens after Nora Leaves Home?

娜 拉 走 后 怎 样

A Talk Given at the Peking Women's Normal College, 26 December 1923

My subject today is: What happens after Nora leaves home?

Ibsen was a Norwegian writer in the second half of the nine-teenth century. All his works, apart from a few dozen poems, are dramas. Most of the dramas he wrote during one period deal with social problems and are known as social-problem plays. One of these is the play *Nora*.[1]

Another title for *Nora* is *Ein Puppenheim*, translated in Chinese as *A Puppet's House*. However, '*puppen*' are not only marionettes but also children's dolls; in a wider sense the term also includes people whose actions are controlled by others. Nora originally lives contentedly in a so-called happy home, but then she wakes up to the fact that she is simply a puppet of her husband's and her children are her puppets. So she leaves home—as the door is heard closing, the curtain falls. Since presumably you all know this play, there is no need to go into details.

What could keep Nora from leaving? Some say that Ibsen himself has supplied the answer in *The Lady from the Sea*. The heroine of this play is married but her former lover, who lives just across the sea, seeks her out suddenly to ask her to elope with him. She tells her husband that she wants to meet this man and finally her husband says, 'I give you complete free-dom. Choose for yourself (whether to go or not). On your own head be it.' This changes everything and she decides not to go. It seems from this that if Nora were to be granted similar freedom she might perhaps stay at home.

But Nora still goes away. What becomes of her afterwards

---

[1] Chinese title for *A Doll's House*.

Ibsen does not say, and now he is dead. Even if he were still living, he would not be obliged to give an answer. For Ibsen was writing poetry, not raising a problem for society and supplying the answer to it. This is like the golden oriole which sings because it wants to, not to amuse or benefit anyone else. Ibsen was rather lacking in worldly wisdom. It is said that when a number of women gave a banquet in his honour and their representative rose to thank him for writing *Nora*, which gave people a new insight into the social consciousness and emancipation of women, he rejoined, 'I didn't write with any such ideas in mind. I was only writing poetry.'

What happens after Nora leaves home? Others have also voiced their views on this. An Englishman has written a play about a modern woman who leaves home but finds no road open to her and therefore goes to the bad, ending up in a brothel. There is also a Chinese—How shall I describe him? A Shanghai man of letters, I suppose—who claims to have read a different version of the play in which Nora returns home in the end. Unfortunately no one else ever saw this edition, unless it was one sent him by Ibsen himself. But by logical deduction, Nora actually has two alternatives only: to go to the bad or to return to her husband. It is like the case of a caged bird: of course there is no freedom in the cage, but if it leaves the cage there are hawks, cats, and other hazards outside; while if imprisonment has atrophied its wings, or if it has forgotten how to fly, there certainly is nowhere it can go. Another alternative is to starve to death, but since that means departing this life it presents no problem and no solution either.

The most painful thing in life is to wake up from a dream and find no way out. Dreamers are fortunate people. If no way out can be seen, the important thing is not to awaken the sleepers. Look at the Tang dynasty poet Li He whose whole life was dogged by misfortune. When he lay dying he said to his mother, 'The Emperor of Heaven has built a palace of white jade, Mother, and summoned me there to write something to celebrate its completion.' What was this if not a lie, a dream? But this made it possible for the young man who was dying to die happily, and for the old woman who lived on to set her heart at rest. At such times there is something great about lying and dreaming. To my mind, then, if we can find no way out, what we need are dreams.

However, it won't do to dream about the future. In one of his novels Artzybashev challenges those idealists who, in order to build a future golden world, call on many people here and now to suffer. 'You promise their descendants a golden world, but what are you giving them themselves?' he demands. Something is given, of course—hope for the future. But the cost is exorbitant. For the sake of this hope, people are made more sensitive to the intensity of their misery, are awakened in spirit to see their own putrid corpses. At such times there is greatness only in lying and dreaming. To my mind, then, if we can find no way out, what we need are dreams; but not dreams of the future, just dreams of the present.

However, since Nora has awakened it is hard for her to return to the dream world; hence all she can do is to leave. After leaving, though, she can hardly avoid going to the bad or returning. Otherwise the question arises: What has she taken away with her apart from her awakened heart? If she has nothing but a crimson woollen scarf of the kind you young ladies are wearing, even if two or three feet wide it will prove completely useless. She needs more than that, needs something in her purse. To put it bluntly, what she needs is money.

Dreams are fine; otherwise money is essential.

The word 'money' has an ugly sound. Fine gentlemen may scoff at it, but I believe that men's views often vary, not only from day to day but from before a meal to after it. All who admit that food costs money yet call money filthy lucre will probably be found, on investigation, to have some fish or pork not yet completely digested in their stomachs. You should hear their views again after they have fasted for a day.

Thus the crucial thing for Nora is money or—to give it a more high-sounding name—economic resources. Of course money cannot buy freedom, but freedom can be sold for money. Human beings have one great drawback, which is that they often get hungry. To remedy this drawback and to avoid being puppets, the most important thing in society today seems to be economic rights. First, there must be a fair sharing out between men and women in the family; secondly, men and women must have equal rights in society.

Unfortunately I have no idea how we are to get hold of these rights; all I know is that we have to fight for them. We may even have to fight harder for these than for political rights.

The demand for economic rights is undoubtedly something very commonplace, yet it may involve more difficulties than the demand for noble political rights or for the grand emancipation of women. In this world countless small actions involve more difficulties than big actions do. In a winter like this, for instance, if we have only a single padded jacket we must choose between saving a poor man from freezing to death or sitting like Buddha under a Bo-tree to ponder ways of saving all mankind. The difference between saving all mankind and saving one individual is certainly vast. But given the choice I would not hesitate to sit down under the Bo-tree, for that would obviate the need to take off my only padded jacket and freeze to death myself. This is why, at home, if you demand political rights you will not meet with much opposition, whereas if you speak about the equal distribution of wealth you will probably find yourself up against enemies, and this of course will lead to bitter fighting.

Fighting is not a good thing and we can't ask everybody to be a fighter. In that case the peaceful method is best, that is using parental authority to liberate one's children in future. Since in China parental authority is absolute, you can share out your property fairly among your children so that they enjoy equal economic rights in peace, free from conflict. They can then go to study, start a business, enjoy themselves, do something for society, or spend the lot just as they please, responsible to no one but themselves. Though this is also a rather distant dream, it is much closer than the dream of a golden age. But the first prerequisite is a good memory. A bad memory is an advantage to its owner but injurious to his descendants. The ability to forget the past enables people to free themselves gradually from the pain they once suffered; but it also often makes them repeat the mistakes of their predecessors. When a cruelly treated daughter-in-law becomes a mother-in-law, she may still treat her daughter-in-law cruelly; officials who detest students were often students who denounced officials; some parents who oppress their children now were probably rebels against their own families ten years ago. This perhaps has something to do with one's age and status; still bad memory is also a big factor here. The remedy for this is for everyone to buy a notebook and record his thoughts and actions from day to day, to serve as reference material in future when his age and status have changed. If you are annoyed with your child for wanting to go to the park, you can look through your notes and find an entry saying: 'I want to go to the Central Park.' This will at once mollify and calm you down. The same applies to other matters too.

There is a kind of hooliganism today, the essence of which is tenacity. It is said that after the Boxer Uprising some ruffians in Tientsin behaved quite lawlessly. For instance, if one were to carry luggage for you, he would demand two dollars. If you argued that it was a small piece of luggage, he would demand two dollars. If you argued that the distance was short, he would demand two dollars. If you said you didn't need him, he would still demand two dollars. Of course hooligans are not good models, yet that tenacity is most admirable. It is the same in demanding economic rights. If someone says this is old hat, tell him you want your economic rights. If he says this is too low, tell him you want your economic rights. If he says the economic system will soon be changing and there is no need to worry, tell him you want your economic rights.

Actually, today, if just one Nora left home she might not find herself in difficulties; because such a case, being so exceptional, would enlist a good deal of sympathy and certain people would help her out. To live on the sympathy of others already means having no freedom; but if a hundred Noras were to leave home, even that sympathy would diminish; while if a thousand or ten thousand were to leave, they would arouse disgust. So having economic power in your own hands is far more reliable.

Are you not a puppet then when you have economic freedom? No, you are still a puppet. But you will be less at the beck and call of others and able to control more puppets yourself. For in present-day society it is not just women who are often the puppets of men; men often control other men, and women other women, while men are often women's puppets too. This is not something which can be remedied by a few women's possession of economic rights. However, people with empty stomachs cannot wait quietly for the arrival of a golden age; they must at least husband their last breath just as a fish in a dry rut flounders about to find a little water. So we need this relatively attainable economic power before we can devise other measures.

Of course, if the economic system changes then all this is empty talk.

In speaking as I have, however, I have assumed Nora to be an ordinary woman. If she is someone exceptional who prefers to dash off to sacrifice herself, that is a different matter. We have no right to urge people to sacrifice themselves, no right to stop them either. Besides, there are many people in the world who delight in self-sacrifice and suffering. In Europe there is a legend that when Jesus was on his way to be crucified he rested under the eaves of Ahasuerus's house, and because Ahasuerus turned Jesus away he became accursed, doomed to find no rest until the Day of Judgment. So since then Ahasuerus has been wandering, unable to rest, and he is still wandering now. Wandering is painful while resting is comfortable, so why doesn't he stop to rest? Because even if under a curse he must prefer wandering to resting; that is why he keeps up this frenzied wandering.

But this choice of sacrifice is a personal one which has nothing in common with the social commitment of revolutionaries. The masses, especially in China, are always spectators at a drama. If the victim on the stage acts heroically, they are watching a tragedy; if he shivers and shakes they are watching a comedy. Before the mutton shops in Peking a few people often gather to gape, with evident enjoyment, at the skinning of the sheep. And this is all they get out of it if a man lays down his life. Moreover, after walking a few steps away from the scene they forget even this modicum of enjoyment.

There is nothing you can do with such people; the only way to save them is to give them no drama to watch. Thus there is no need for spectacular sacrifices; it is better to have persistent, tenacious struggle.

Unfortunately China is very hard to change. Just to move a

table or overhaul a stove probably involves shedding blood;
and even so, the change may not get made. Unless some great
whip lashes her on the back, China will never budge. Such a
whip is bound to come, I think. Whether good or bad, this
whipping is bound to come. But where it will come from or how
it will come I do not know exactly.

And here my talk ends.

On Deferring 'Fair Play'

论 " 费 厄 泼 赖 " 应 该 缓 行

1 *Broaching the subject*

In Number 57 of *The Tatler* Mr. Lin Yutang refers to 'fair play',
and remarks that since this spirit is extremely rare in China we
should do our best to encourage it. He adds that 'Don't beat
a dog in the water' supplements the meaning of 'fair play'. Not
knowing English, I do not understand the full connotation of
this term; but if 'Don't beat a dog in the water' represents the
true spirit of fair play, then I must beg to differ. In order not
to offend the eye—not to 'add false antlers to my head',[1] I
mean—I did not state this explicitly in my title. What I mean,
anyway, is this: a dog in the water may—or rather should—be
beaten.

2 *On three kinds of dog in the water which should be beaten*

Modern critics often compare 'beating a dead tiger' with
'beating a dog in the water', considering both as somewhat
cowardly. I find those who pose as brave by beating dead tigers
rather amusing. They may be cowards, but in an engaging way.
Beating a dog in the water is not such a simple issue, however.
You must first see what sort of dog it is and how it fell in. There
are three chief reasons for a dog's falling into the water:

         1) It may fall in by mistake.
         2) It may be pushed in by someone.
         3) It may be pushed in by you.

In the first two cases, of course, it is pointless if not cowardly
to join in beating the dog. But if you are in a fight with a dog
and have pushed it into the water, then to give it a good beating

---

[1] Professor Chen Yuan accused Lu Xun of doing this in order to pose as a fighter.

again in the water with a bamboo pole is not too much, for this is different from the two other cases.

They say that a brave prize-fighter never hits his opponent when he is down, and that this sets a fine example for us all. But I agree to this only on condition that the opponent is a brave pugilist too; for then once he is beaten he will be ashamed to come back, or will come back openly to take his revenge, either of which is all right. But this does not apply to dogs, who cannot be considered in the same class; for however wildly they may bark they really have no sense of 'propriety'. Besides, a dog can swim and will certainly swim ashore. If you are not careful it will shake itself, spattering water all over you, then run away with its tail between its legs. But next time it will do exactly the same. Simple souls may think that falling into the water is a kind of baptism, after which a dog will surely repent of its sins and never bite men again. They could hardly be more mistaken.

So I think all dogs that bite men should be beaten, whether they are on the land or in the water.

3 *Pugs, in particular, must be pushed into the water and soundly beaten*

Pugs or pekes are called Western dogs in south China, but I understand this is a special Chinese breed. At international dog shows they often win gold medals, and a number of the photographs of dogs in the *Encyclopaedia Britannica* are pictures of our Chinese pugs. This is also a national honour. Now dogs and cats are mortal enemies, but this pug, although a dog, looks very much like a cat, so moderate, affable, and self-possessed, its smug air seeming to say: 'Everyone else goes to extremes, but I practise the Doctrine of the Mean.' That is why it is such a favourite with influential persons, eunuchs, and the wives and daughters of rich men, and its line remains unbroken. It is kept by top people because it looks so cute, and its function is to patter after Chinese or foreign ladies with a tiny chain attached to its neck when they go shopping.

These dogs should be pushed into the water, then soundly beaten. If they fall into the water themselves, there is no harm in beating them either. Of course, if you are over-scrupulous,

you need not beat them; but neither need you feel sorry for
them. If you can forgive these dogs, there is no call for you to
beat any other dogs; for though the others also fawn on the rich
and bully the poor, they at least look something like wolves and
are rather wild—not such fence-sitters as these pugs.

But this is just a digression, which may not have much
bearing on the main subject.

4 On the harm done to posterity by not beating dogs in the water

So whether or not a dog in the water should be beaten depends
first of all on its attitude after it crawls ashore.

It is hard for a dog to change its nature. Ten thousand years
from now it may be somewhat different, but I am talking about
today. If we think it looks pathetic in the water, so do many
other pests. And though cholera germs breed so fast, they look
very tame; yet doctors show them no mercy.

Present-day officials and Chinese or foreign-style gentlemen
call everything that does not suit them 'Red' or 'Bolshevik'.
Before 1912 it was slightly different: first they referred to
Kang Youwei's partisans as undesirables, then revolutionaries,
and even informed against them. They were trying, for one
thing, to keep their high position, but they may also have
wanted 'to stain their cap-button red with human blood'.[1]
But at last the revolution came, and those gentlemen with their
high and mighty airs suddenly panicked like homeless curs and
wound up their little queues on their heads. And the revolutionaries were very up-to-date, very 'civilized' in a way these
gentlemen detested. They said: 'The revolution is for all. We
will not beat a dog in the water: let it crawl ashore.' This was
just what the others did. They lay low till the second half of
1913 and the time of the second revolution, then suddenly came
forward to help Yuan Shikai kill many revolutionaries, so
that things became daily worse in China again. Thus now,
besides the old die-hards, there are many young ones. This
is thanks to those martyrs who were too kind to these snakes in
the grass and allowed them to multiply. The young people who

[1] In the Qing dynasty, mandarins of the first rank had a coral bead on their
caps. Some officials killed revolutionaries in order to gain promotion.

understand this will have to strive much harder and sacrifice many more lives to oppose the forces of darkness.

Qiu Jin[1] died at the hands of these informers. Just after the revolution she was called a heroine, but this term is rarely heard now. When the revolution started, a general—what we would call a 'warlord' today—came to her district and he was her comrade. His name was Wang Jinfa. He arrested the man responsible for her death and collected evidence to avenge her. But in the end he let the informer go because—so they say—the Republic had been founded and bygones should be bygones. When the second revolution was defeated, however, Wang was shot by Yuan Shikai's stooge; and the man who brought about Qiu Jin's death and whom Wang had set free had a great deal to do with this.

Since then this informer has died peacefully in bed. But because there are still many of his sort lording it in that district, Qiu Jin's native place has remained unchanged from year to year, and made no progress at all. From this point of view, Miss Yang Yinyu and Professor Chen Yuan are really supremely fortunate to come from China's 'model district'.[2]

5 *Those who have fallen from power are not the same as dogs in the water*

Passive resistance is merciful. 'An eye for an eye and a tooth for a tooth' is just. In China, however, most things are topsy-turvy: instead of beating dogs in the water, we let ourselves be bitten by them. This is simply asking for trouble like fools.

'Kindness is another name for folly,' says the proverb. This may be going too far. Yet if you think carefully, this is not intended to lead men astray, but is the conclusion reached after many bitter experiences. There may be two reasons for the reluctance to hit a dog when it has fallen into the water: it is either because we are not strong enough, or because we have made a false analogy. We need not go into the first possibility. As regards the second, we can find two serious flaws. First, we make the mistake of considering dogs in the water as the same

---

[1] (1875–1907). A woman revolutionary who was one of the leaders of the anti-Manchu movement. In 1907 she was arrested and killed in Shaoxing.

[2] Wusih, described as 'a model district' by Chen Yuan.

as men who have come down in the world. Secondly, we make the mistake of considering all those who have fallen from power as alike, without drawing a distinction between the good and the bad. The result is that evil-doers go unpunished. At present, for instance, since the political situation is unstable, men rise and fall all the time. Relying on some short-lived authority, a bad man may commit any crime he pleases, until one day he falls and has to beg for mercy. Then simple souls who have known him or suffered at his hands consider him a dog in the water, and instead of beating him feel sorry for him. They imagine justice has already been done and they may as well be chivalrous, unaware that the dog is not really in the water, but has long since prepared its hide-out and laid in food in the foreign concessions. Sometimes it may look hurt, but this is put on: it pretends to limp to enlist sympathy, so that it can go into hiding comfortably. It will come out later and make a fresh start by biting simple souls, then go on to commit all manner of crimes. And the reason for this is partly that those simple souls would not beat a dog in the water. So, strictly speaking, they are digging their own graves, and they have no right to blame fate or other people.

6 *We cannot yet afford to be too fair*

Humanitarians may ask: In that case, don't we want fair play at all? I can answer this at once: Of course we do, but not yet. This is using their own argument. Though humanitarians may not be willing to use it, I can make out a case for it. Do not Chinese and foreign-style gentlemen often say that China's special features make foreign ideas of liberty and equality unsuitable for us? I take this to include fair play. Otherwise, if a man is unfair to you but you are fair to him, you will suffer for it in the end: not only will you fail to get fair treatment, but it will be too late to be unfair yourself. So before being fair, you have to know your opponent. If he does not deserve fair treatment, you had better not be polite. Only when he is fair can you talk to him of fair play.

This sounds rather like a proposal for a dual morality, but I cannot help it; for without this China will never have a better future. The dual morality here takes many forms: different standards for masters and for slaves, for men and for women. It would be quite unrealistic and premature to treat dogs in the water and men in the water as the same. This is the argument of those gentlemen who say that while freedom and equality are good, in China it is still too early for them. So if anyone wants indiscriminate fair play, I suggest we wait till those dogs in the water are more human. Of course, this does not mean that fair play cannot be practised at all at present; the important thing, as I have just said, is first to know your opponent. And a certain discrimination is required. In other words, your fairness must depend on who your opponent is. Never mind how he has fallen into the water, if he is a man we should help him; if a dog, we should ignore him; if a bad dog, we should beat him. In brief, we should befriend our own kind and attack our enemies.

We need not trouble ourselves just now with the aphorisms of those gentlemen who have justice on their lips but self-interest in their hearts. Even the justice so loudly demanded by honest folk cannot help good people in China today, but may actually protect the bad instead. For when bad men are in power and ill-treat the good, however loudly someone calls for justice they will certainly not listen to him. His cry is simply a cry, and the good continue to suffer. But if the good happen for once to come out on top while the bad fall into the water, those honest upholders of justice shout: 'Don't take vengeance! ... Be magnanimous! ... Don't oppose evil with evil!' And this time their outcry takes effect instead of going unheeded; for the good agree with them, and the bad are spared. After being spared, though, they simply congratulate themselves on their luck instead of repenting. Besides, they have prepared hide-outs in advance, and are good at worming their way into favour; so in no time they become as powerful and as vicious as before. When this happens, the upholders of justice may raise another outcry but this time it will not be heard.

Nevertheless it is true that when reformers are over-zealous, like the scholars at the end of the Han dynasty or those of the Ming dynasty, they defeat their own ends. Indeed, this is the criticism usually levelled against them. But though the other side detest good folk, nobody reproaches them for it. If there is no fight to the finish between darkness and light, and simple souls go on making the mistake of confusing forgiveness with giving free rein to evil, and continue pardoning wicked men, then the present state of chaos will last for ever.

7 On dealing with them as they deal with others

Some Chinese believe in traditional Chinese medicine, others in Western medicine, and both types of doctors can now be found in our larger towns, so that patients may take their choice. I thoroughly approve of this. If this were applied more generally, I am sure there would be fewer complaints, and perhaps we could even secure peace and prosperity. For instance, the usual form of greeting now is to bow; but if anyone disapproves of this, he can kowtow instead. The new penal code has no punishment by bastinado; but if anyone approves of corporal punishment when he breaks the law he can have his bottom specially spanked. Bowls, chopsticks, and cooked food are the custom today; but if anyone hankers after ancient times, he can eat raw meat. We can also build several thousand thatched huts, and move all those fine gentlemen who so admire the age of Yao and Shun[1] out of their big houses to live there; while those who oppose material civilization should certainly not be compelled to travel in cars. When this is done, there will be no more complaints, for everyone will be satisfied, and we shall enjoy peace and quiet.

But the pity is that nobody will do this. Instead, they judge others by themselves, and hence there is all this trouble in the world. Fair play is particularly liable to cause trouble, and may even be made use of by the forces of evil. For example, when Liu Baizhao[2] beat up and carried off students of the Women's Normal College, there was not so much as a squeak from *Modern Review*. But when the buildings were recovered, and Professor Chen Yuan encouraged the students of the Women's University to stay on in the dormitories, the journal said: 'Suppose they don't want to go? Surely you aren't going to carry off their things by force?' If they remained silent the first

[1] Two legendary Chinese rulers of the earliest times, described in old books as living in thatched huts.

[2] In 1925 the Minister of Education, Zhang Shizhao, disbanded the Women's Normal College and set up a new Women's University in the same premises under Liu Baizhao. Liu used strong-arm methods to take over.

time, when Liu Baizhao beat up students and carried things away, how was it that this time they felt it would not do? It was because they felt there was fair play in the Women's Normal College. But this fair play had become a bad thing, since it was utilized to protect the followers of Zhang Shizhao.

8 *Conclusion*

I may be accused of stirring up trouble by this argument between the old and the new or some other schools of thought, and of aggravating their enmity and sharpening the conflict between them. But I can state with certainty that those who oppose reform have never relaxed their efforts to injure reformers, and have always done their worst. It is only the reformers who are asleep, and always suffer for it. That is why China has never had reforms. From now on we should modify our attitude and our tactics.

29 December 1925

Silent China　　　无 声 的 中 国

A Talk Given at the Hongkong Y.M.C.A., 16 February 1927

First of all, I want to express my respectful appreciation to all of you who have come through this downpour to hear one of my empty and futile talks.

My subject today is Silent China.

There is fighting now in Chekiang and Shensi, but we do not know whether folk there are laughing or crying. Hongkong seems very quiet, but outsiders do not know whether the Chinese who live here are comfortable or not.

Men communicate their thoughts and feelings through writing, yet most Chinese nowadays are still unable to express themselves this way. This is not our fault, for our written language is a fearful legacy left us by our forebears. Even after years of effort, it is hard to write. And because it is hard, many people simply ignore it. A man may not be sure which character Zhang his name is, or may not be able to write his name at all, only to say it. Although he can speak, not many can hear him; so those at a distance are left in ignorance, and this is tantamount to silence. Again, because it is hard, some regard it as a treasure and amuse themselves by using erudite terms which only a small minority understands. We cannot be sure, indeed, that even this minority understands; and since the great majority certainly does not, this too is tantamount to silence.

One of the differences between civilized men and savages is that civilized men have writing to convey their thoughts and feelings to the rest of the world and to posterity. China also has writing, but a writing quite divorced from the mass of the people. Couched in crabbed, archaic language, it describes outmoded, archaic sentiments. All its utterances belong to the past, and therefore amount to nothing. Hence our people, unable to understand each other, are like a great dish of loose sand.

It may be amusing to treat writing as a curio—the fewer who know and understand it the better. But what is the result? Already we are unable to express our feelings. Injured or insulted, we cannot retort as we should. Consider, for instance, such recent happenings in China as the Sino-Japanese War, the Boxer Rebellion, and the 1911 Revolution. All these were major events, yet so far not one good work on them has appeared. Nor has anyone spoken out since the Republic was founded. Abroad, on the other hand, references are constantly being made to China—but by foreigners, not by Chinese.

This dumbness was not so serious during the Ming dynasty, when Chinese expressed themselves comparatively better. But when the alien Manchus invaded our country they killed all who talked about history—especially late Song history [1]—and those, of course, who talked about current events. Thus by the reign of Qian Long, men no longer dared express themselves in writing. So-called scholars took refuge in studying the classics, collating and reprinting old books, and writing a little in the ancient style on subjects quite unrelated to their own time. New ideas were taboo: you wrote like either Han Yu [2] or Su Dongpo. [3] These men were quite all right in their own way—they said what needed to be said about their own time. But how can we, who are not living in the Tang or Song dynasty, write in the style of an age so far removed from our own? Even if the imitation is convincing, the voice is from the Tang or Song dynasty, the voice of Han Yu or Su Dongpo, not the voice of our generation. But Chinese today are still playing this same old game. We have men but no voices, and how lonely that is! Can men be silent? No, not unless they are dead, or—to put it more politely—when they are dumb.

To restore speech to this China which has been silent for centuries is not an easy matter. It is like ordering a dead man to live again. Though I know nothing of religion, I fancy this approximates to what believers call a 'miracle'.

---

[1] The Song dynasty was overthrown by northern Tartars. The Manchus suppressed critical discussion of earlier barbarian conquests of China.

[2] (768–824), a prose writer of the Tang dynasty.

[3] (1036–1101), a poet of the Song dynasty.

The first to attempt this was Dr. Hu Shi, who a year before the May Fourth Movement advocated a 'literary revolution'. I do not know if you are frightened of the word 'revolution' here, but in some places people are terrified of it. However, this literary 'revolution' is not as fearful as the French Revolution. It simply means a reform, and once we substitute the word 'reform', it sounds quite inoffensive. So let us do that. The Chinese language is very ingenious in this way. All we want is this: instead of overtaxing our brains to learn the speech of men long since dead, we should speak that of living men. Instead of treating language as a curio, we should write in the easily understood vernacular. A simple literary reform is not enough, though, for corrupt ideas can be conveyed in the vernacular just as well as in classical Chinese. This is why a reform of ideas was later proposed. And this led to a movement for social reform. As soon as this started, opposition sprang up and a battle began to rage.

In China, the mere mention of literary reform is enough to arouse opposition. Still, the vernacular gradually gained ground, and met with fewer obstacles. How was this? It was because Mr. Qian Xuantong[1] was at the same time proposing to abolish Chinese ideographs and romanize the language. This would have been merely a normal language reform, but when our die-hard Chinese heard of it, they thought the end of the world had come and hastily passed the relatively inoffensive literary reform in order to devote all their energies to abusing Qian Xuantong. The vernacular took advantage of this to spread, since it now had far fewer opponents and less obstacles in its way.

By temperament the Chinese love compromise and a happy mean. For instance, if you say this room is too dark and a window should be made, everyone is sure to disagree. But if you propose taking off the roof, they will compromise and be glad to make a window. In the absence of more drastic proposals, they will never agree to the most inoffensive reforms. The vernacular was able to spread only because of the proposal to abolish Chinese characters and use a romanized alphabet.

[1] Professor at Peking University and a contributor to *New Youth* during the May Fourth movement.

In fact, the time has long since passed for canvassing the respective merits of the classical language and the vernacular; but China abhors quick decisions, and many futile debates are still going on. Some, for instance, say: Classical Chinese is comprehensible in every province, whereas the vernacular varies from place to place and cannot be understood throughout the country. But, as everyone knows, once we have universal education and better communications, the whole country will understand the more intelligible vernacular. As for the classical language, it is not comprehensible to everyone in every province, but only to a few. Others argue that if everyone uses the vernacular, we shall not be able to read the classics, and Chinese culture will perish. The fact is, we of this generation had much better not read the classics. There is no need to be alarmed—if the classics really contain anything of value, they can be translated into the vernacular. Yet others urge that since foreigners have translated our classics, thus proving their worth, we ought to read them ourselves. But, as everyone knows, foreigners have also translated the hieroglyphic texts of the Egyptians and the myths of the African Negroes. They do so from ulterior motives, and to be translated by them is no great honour.

Recently others have argued that since thought reform is what matters, while language reform is secondary, it is better to use clear, simple, classical language to convey the new ideas, to arouse less opposition. This sounds like sense. But we know that the men unwilling to cut their long fingernails[1] will never cut their queues.

Because we use the language of the ancients, which the people cannot understand and do not hear, we are like a dish of loose sand—oblivious to each other's sufferings. The first necessity, if we want to come to life, is for our young people to stop speaking the language of Confucius and Mencius, Han Yu, and Liu Zongyuan.[2] This is a different era, and times have changed. Hongkong was not like this in the time of Confucius,

---

[1] Towards the end of the Qing dynasty it was fashionable for scholars to wear their nails very long. To cut their nails might have been bold; but to cut off their queues would have been a declaration of rebellion.

[2] (773–819), a prose writer of the Tang dynasty.

and we cannot use the old sage's language to write on Hongkong. Such phrases as 'Hongkong, how great thou art!' are simply nonsense.

We must speak our own language, the language of today, using the living vernacular to give clear expression to our thoughts and feelings. Of course, we shall be jeered at for this by our elders and betters, who consider the vernacular vulgar and worthless, and say young writers are childish and will make fools of themselves. But how many in China can write the classical language? The rest can only use the vernacular. Do you mean to say that all these Chinese are vulgar and worthless? As for childishness, that is nothing to be ashamed of, any more than children need be ashamed of comparison with grown-ups. The childish can grow and mature; and as long as they do not become decrepit and corrupt, all will be well. As for waiting till you are mature before making a move, not even a country woman would be so foolish. If her child falls down while learning to walk, she does not order him to stay in bed until he has mastered the art of walking.

First our young people must turn China into an articulate country. Speak out boldly, advance fearlessly, with no thought of personal gain, brushing aside the ancients, and expressing your true thoughts. Of course, to be truthful is far from easy. It is not easy to be truly oneself, for instance. When I make a speech I am not truly myself—for I talk differently to children or to my friends. Still, we can talk in a relatively truthful way and express relatively truthful ideas. And only then shall we be able to move the people of China and the world. Only then shall we be able to live in the world with all the other nations.

Let us think which are the nations today which are silent. Can we hear the voice of the Egyptian people? Can we hear the Annamese or the Koreans? Is there any voice raised in India but that of Tagore?

There are only two paths open to us. One is to cling to our classical language and die; the other is to cast that language aside and live.

Hongkong Again   再 谈 香 港

28 September was the third time I passed through Hongkong, a place I dread.

The first time I had a little luggage, but nothing happened. The second time I had no luggage, and I have written something[1] about what happened. This time I believe I felt more uneasy than on either of those occasions, for I had read Mr. Wang Duqing's letter in *Creation Monthly* describing how those Chinese compatriots employed by the British throw their weight about when they board a ship to examine the passengers' luggage, cursing and beating people, or demanding a few dollars from them. And I had ten cases of books in the saloon, as well as six cases of books and clothes in my cabin.

Of course, it would be an experience to see how my compatriots behaved under the British flag, but I feared it would prove a costly one. Just to repack all those cases after they had been through them would take plenty of time. If I wanted to make an experiment, I should have taken one or two pieces only. Still, it was too late now. What must be must be. But should I pay up or let them go through all the cases? If they searched them all, how was I to repack single-handed?

Our boat reached Hongkong on the 28th, and nothing happened that day. The next afternoon a steward hurried up and beckoned me outside the cabin.

'Customs examination,' he said. 'Go and open your cases.'

I took my keys to the saloon. Sure enough, two British compatriots in dark green uniforms were standing by my pile

---

[1] Lu Xun first visited Hongkong on his way from Amoy to Canton in January 1927. He returned the next month to address some students (see 'Silent China', p. 163), and in July wrote an article 'On Hongkong' published the next month in the *Tatler*.

of cases, wielding pointed iron rods. I told them there was
nothing inside but old books, yet they did not seem to understand. They rapped out three words only:

'Open them up!'

'That's right,' I thought. 'How can they take the word of a
perfect stranger?'

Of course the cases must be opened, so with the help of two
stewards I opened them.

The moment the search started, I realized that the Hongkong
customs officers were not like those in Canton. When I left
Canton my luggage was examined too. But the officers there
looked human and understood what I said. After taking out a
bundle of papers or books, they would put it back where it
came from without mixing everything up. That was the way to
look through things. But it was very different in Hongkong, this
'paradise of the British'. The customs officers here were pale as
ghosts and did not seem to understand me. They emptied out
the contents of one of my cases and rummaged among them.
Whenever they found a package, they tore off the wrappings.
After undergoing this treatment, the books overtopped the case
by six or seven inches.

Then we came to the second case.

'Open it up!'

'I may as well have a try,' I thought.

'Must you open it?' I whispered to one of them.

'Give me ten dollars,' he whispered back. So he did understand me.

'Two dollars.'

I wouldn't have minded paying more, for this type of
examination was terrible: to repack ten cases would take me
at least five hours. Unfortunately I had only two one-dollar
notes. All my other notes were for ten dollars, but I did not
want to part with them yet.

'Open it up!'

Two stewards carried my second case to the deck, and he
went through the same procedure. Again one case of books
became one case and a half, and several thick bundles of papers
were also torn up. We bargained as he searched. I raised my
offer to five, but he refused to come down below seven. By this

time we were at the fifth case, and a crowd had gathered to watch the fun.

Since he had opened half the cases, I thought he might as well look at them all. So I stopped negotiating, and nothing was said except 'Open it up!' But my two compatriots seemed to be losing interest, for by degrees they stopped looking through everything, and just pulled twenty or thirty books out to throw on top of each case, then marked it 'Passed'. A bundle of old letters appeared to arouse their interest and revive their spirits, but after reading four or five they set these aside too. I believe they opened one more case after that, then left this welter of books, and that was that.

I saw now that eight cases had been opened, two had been left untouched. And these two unscathed cases held books belonging to Fuyuan which I was taking to Shanghai for him. All my own were in an unholy mess.

'Some people are born lucky, and Fuyuan is one of them!' I thought. 'But I haven't come to the end of my bad luck yet. Ah, well . . .' I squatted down to pick up some of the scattered books, but had hardly collected any before another steward shouted at me from the door.

'Customs examination in your cabin! Go and open your cases.'

Entrusting the repacking of my books to the saloon stewards, I ran back to my cabin. True, two British compatriots were there waiting for me. The bedding on my bunk was thoroughly rumpled, and a stool was lying on top of it. As soon as I went in, they searched my wallet. I thought they wanted to see my visiting-cards to find out my name, but instead of looking at my cards they looked at my two ten-dollar notes, then gave them back to me and told me to be careful of them, as if they were afraid I might lose them.

Next they opened my suitcase which was full of clothes, and shook out only about a dozen garments which they tossed on the bed. Next they examined my basket, and found seven silver dollars wrapped in paper. Having unwrapped these and counted them, they fell silent. There was another package containing ten dollars, but being further down that escaped their notice. Next they examined my handkerchief which lay

on a bench, and in which were a package of ten dollars' worth
of small silver coins, four or five dollars in loose silver, and
several dozen coppers. Having examined these, they fell silent
again. Next they turned to my portmanteau. This time I had
quite a fright. I was a little slow in producing the key, but
luckily just as my compatriots were raising their iron rods to
smash the lock it was ready. I was able to breathe again. This
portmanteau also held clothes and these, it goes without saying,
were shaken out in the usual way.

'Give us ten dollars and we won't search you,' said one
compatriot as he went through my portmanteau.

I picked up some loose silver in a handkerchief and offered
it to him, but he would not take it. He turned away and went
on with his search.

Now for a short digression. While this compatriot was
examining my suitcase and portmanteau, the other was examining my net-basket. He had a different method from that used to
look through books in the saloon. Then they simply created
chaos, now he destroyed. First he tore up the carton from a
bottle of cod-liver oil and threw it to the floor, then with his iron
rod he bored a hole in the canister of litchi-scented tea given me
by Mr. Jiang Jingsan. While boring this hole his roving eye
fell on a small knife on the table. I had purchased this for a few
coppers at the White Dagoba Temple Fair in Peking, and taken
it to Canton where I peeled carambolas with it. I measured it
later, and it was 5·3 inches long, including the handle. Still,
he said I was guilty of a serious offence.

'Here is a dangerous weapon. This is a serious offence.' He
pointed the small knife at me.

When I said nothing, he put the small knife down and poked
a hole in a packet of salted peanuts. Then he picked up a box
of mosquito incense.

'What is this?'

'Mosquito incense,' I said. 'Don't you see the name on the
box?'

'No. This looks suspicious.'

He took out one stick of the incense and sniffed at it. I do
not know what he did next, because the other one had finished
with one case of clothes and wanted me to open another case.

This time I was worried, for the second case held not clothes or books but photographs, manuscripts, some of my translations and my friends', as well as news cuttings, reference material, and other odds and ends. It would be too bad if these were destroyed or mixed up. But just at this point that compatriot walked over to have another look at the handkerchief with money in it. At that I saw light, and boldly picked up the silver coins in the handkerchief—ten dollars' worth—and showed them to him. He looked outside the door, reached out for the money, marked the second case as passed, then went over to the other compatriot. He must have made a sign to him, but strange to say he did not take the money, simply tucked it under my pillow and went out.

All this time the other compatriot was jabbing viciously with his iron rod at a jar of biscuits. I thought after being given the secret sign he would stop, but no. He went on with his work, opened the sealed jar, threw the wooden lid on the floor and broke it in two, took out a biscuit, crumbled it, dropped it into the jar, and then finally sauntered off.

Peace reigned again. As I sat amid the shambles in my cabin, I realized that my compatriots had not made trouble to begin with out of spite. For even if we agreed on a figure, a little damage must be done first for the sake of appearances: the chaos showed that there had been an examination. Did not Mr. Wang Duqing point out that over these compatriots was a big-nosed white boss? This must have been why the customs officer looked out before taking the money. But I had not seen this boss.

The later destruction did show some spite though. I suppose it was my fault for giving them loose silver instead of banknotes, for those silver coins would make a bulge in a uniform pocket and could be detected by the boss. That is why he had to leave them for the time being under the pillow. No doubt he would collect them when his work was done.

The tramp of leather shoes drew near and stopped outside my door. I looked up and saw a white man, rather stout, doubtless the boss of those two compatriots.

'Examination over?' he asked, beaming.

Yes, indeed, that was the voice of the boss. But it was so

obvious, why ask? Perhaps he wanted to commiserate because my luggage was in a special mess, or perhaps he was laughing at me.

He picked up a pictorial supplement of *The China Press* outside the cabin. I had used it as a wrapper, but my compatriots had torn it off and thrown it there. After leaning against the wall to read it, he passed slowly on.

I thought since the boss had passed, the examination must be over, so I repacked the first case.

But this was premature. Another compatriot came in and said, 'Open it up.' The following dialogue ensued.

'He has already seen it,' I said.

'Who has? This hasn't been opened. Open it up!'

'I've only just closed it.'

'You don't say! Open it up!'

'Isn't this the sign showing it's been passed?'

'Ha, so you gave him money, eh? Using bribes . . .'

'. . .'

'How much did you give him?'

'Go and ask your people.'

He left. And soon the other hurried in and took the money from under the pillow. That was the last I saw of them—now peace really reigned.

Then I slowly repacked my belongings. I saw a few things grouped together on the table: one pair of scissors, one tin-opener, and one small knife with a wooden handle. If not for the ten dollars' worth of small silver coins, these would no doubt have been considered as 'dangerous weapons' and used with the 'suspicious' incense to threaten me. But that stick of incense had gone.

When the ship cast off everything seemed quieter. A steward came to chat with me, but he blamed me for all the ransacking of my luggage.

'You are too thin,' he explained. 'They suspected you of smuggling opium.'

I was really flabbergasted. It is true that 'human life is short, but knowledge is infinite'. I had thought that if you competed for a rice-bowl you would get knocked on the head, but that it was all right to give one up; however last year in

Amoy I learned that while having a rice-bowl is hard, refusing one also annoys 'scholars', who then criticize you for insubordination. I long ago learned what a ticklish business it is to grow a moustache, with the differences between Chinese and Western styles. But this year in Canton I learned that even the colour is restricted, for someone wrote to the paper to warn me not to let my moustache turn grey or red. As for this prohibition on thinness, I only learned it after going to Hongkong—I had never dreamed of it before.

It is true, that Westerner supervising my compatriots in the customs was really very well-nourished.

Though Hongkong is just one island, it gives a true picture of many parts of China today and in time to come. At the centre are a few foreign bosses, with some 'high-class Chinese' under them to praise their virtue, and some slavish compatriots to act as their stooges. All the rest are 'natives' who suffer in silence. Those who acquiesce die in the foreign concessions, while those who will not acquiesce escape into the deep mountains, as the Miaos and the Yaos[1] did long ago.

The night of 29 September, at sea
1927

[1] Minority peoples driven from central China to the mountains in the southwest.

The Revolutionary Literature of the Chinese Proletariat and the Blood of the Pioneers

中 国 无 产 阶 级 革 命 文 学 和

前 驱 的 血

The revolutionary literature of the Chinese proletariat, coming into being as today passes over into tomorrow, is growing amid slander and persecution. Now at last in the utter darkness its first chapter has been written with our comrades' blood.[1]

Throughout history our toiling masses have been so bitterly oppressed and exploited that even the boon of a schooling was denied them. They could only suffer slaughter and destruction in silence. And our ideographic script is so difficult that they have no chance to learn to read themselves. Once our young intellectuals realized their duty as pioneers they were the first to raise a battle-cry, a cry which terrified the rulers as much as the cries of revolt of the toiling masses themselves. Then hack-writers rallied to the attack, spread rumours or acted as informers. And the fact that they always operated in secret and under false names simply proves them creatures of darkness.

Since the rulers knew their hack-writers were no match for the revolutionary literature of the proletariat, they started banning books and periodicals, closing bookshops, issuing repressive publishing laws, and black-listing authors. And now they have resorted to the lowest tactics of all, arresting and imprisoning left-wing writers and putting them to death in secret—to this day they have not made these 'executions' public. While this proves them creatures of darkness on the verge of extinction, it also testifies to the strength of the camp of revolutionary literature of the Chinese proletariat. For as their obituaries show, the age, courage, and, above all, the

[1] On 17 January 1931 Rou Shi, Bai Mang, and three other young members of the League of Left-Wing Writers were arrested by the Kuomintang authorities. On 7 February they were secretly murdered at night in Shanghai.

literary achievements of our martyred comrades were enough to stop the frenzied yapping of the whole pack of curs.

But now these comrades of ours have been murdered. This naturally represents a certain loss to the revolutionary literature of the working class and a great grief to us. Yet our proletarian literature will continue to grow, because it belongs to the broad masses of revolutionary toilers; and as long as the people exist and gain in strength, so long will this revolutionary literature grow. Our comrades' blood testifies that the revolutionary literature of the working class is subjected to the same oppression and terror as the toiling masses, that it is fighting the same battles and shares the same destiny, that it is the literature of the revolutionary toilers

Now according to the warlords, even old ladies of sixty have been poisoned by 'noxious writing', and the police in the foreign concessions are periodically searching even primary-school children. Apart from the guns given them by the imperialists and apart from a few toadies, the diehards have nothing left, nothing but enemies. Old folk and children alike are all against them, not to mention the youth. And these enemies of theirs are all on our side.

As with bitter grief in our hearts we commemorate our fallen comrades today, we must impress on our memories that the first page in the history of the revolutionary literature of China's proletariat has been written with our comrades' blood. It is a lasting exposure of the enemy's contemptible savagery, an inspiration to us never to cease our struggle.

1931

The Secret of Being a Joker

帮 闲 法 发 隐

Kierkegaard is a Dane with a gloomy outlook on life, whose works always breathe indignation. But he says some amusing things too, as in the passage below:

A theatre catches fire. The clown steps to the front of the stage to announce the fact to the audience, who think it a joke and applaud. Then the clown announces again that there is a fire, but they roar with laughter and clap more loudly than ever. No doubt the world will end amid the general applause of these laughter-loving people who take everything as a joke.

What amuses me, however, is not this passage alone but the way it reminds me of these jokers' cunning. When there is work to be done, they help out. When their masters are bent on crime, they become accomplices. But they help in such a way that in case of bloodshed no bloodstain is found on them, nor any smell of blood.

For instance, if something serious has happened and everyone is taking it seriously, the joker starts clowning to make the thing look funny, or exaggerates some irrelevant aspects of it to distract attention. This is known as 'playing the fool'. If murder has been done, he describes the scene of the crime and the hard work of the detectives. If the one killed is a woman, so much the better: he can refer to her as 'the lovely corpse' or introduce her diary. If it is an assassination, he tells the life story of the victim, relates his love affairs and the anecdotes about him. . . . Passions are bound to cool down eventually, but cold water—or, to be more refined, 'green tea'—will speed up the cooling-off process. Then this fellow playing the fool becomes a man of letters.

If a serious alarm is raised before men have grown completely apathetic, of course that is bad for the murderer. But then the joker can play the fool again, cracking jokes and making faces on one side, so that the man who has raised the alarm looks like a clown himself to everyone, and his warnings sound laughable. The joker shrinks and shivers to show how rich and mighty the other is. He bows and sighs to show the other's pride. Then the man who raised the alarm is considered a hypocrite. Luckily most of these jokers are men: otherwise they could accuse the one who gives the warning of attempted seduction, make public a great many indecent details, and finally pretend to kill themselves for shame. When there are jokers all around, the most serious talk loses its force and amid the suspicion and laughter an end is made of everything unfavourable to the murderer. This time the joker appears as a moralist.

When there are no incidents of this kind, jokers collect tittle-tattle for the newspaper supplements every week or ten days with which to stuff readers' heads. After reading this for six months or a year, your mind is stocked with stories of how a certain great man plays mah-jong or a certain film star sneezes. This is naturally quite amusing. But the world will come to an end amid the laughter of these laughter-loving people.

28 August 1933

The Case of Mrs. Qin Lizhai

论 秦 理 斋 夫 人 事

The last few years have seen many accounts in the papers of suicides due to economic pressure or social taboos, but such cases are seldom discussed or written up. However, the recent suicide of Mrs. Qin Lizhai[1] and her two sons and daughter has given rise to not a little comment, and the subsequent suicide of a man who had an account of their death beside him[2] shows even better the scope of its influence. I fancy this was because of the number involved. A single suicide is not enough to excite general sympathy.

Although all the comments express some compassion for the principal suicide—Mrs. Qin—in the final analysis they still condemn her. For though the society is bad, say the commentators, man's first duty is to live and suicide means shirking this responsibility; man's second duty is to suffer, and suicide means taking the easy way out. Progressive commentators declare that human life is a battle and suicide desertion, for which death is not sufficient to atone. Although there is truth in this statement, it is rather too sweeping.

There are two schools of criminologists, the first of whom ascribe crime to the environment, the second to individual nature. At present the second is in the ascendant; for if we believed the first, to wipe out crime we must change the environment and that would be a troublesome, fearful business. Most of the critics of Mrs. Qin's suicide belong to the second school.

---

[1] The wife of a member of the staff of the *Shen Bao* who died on 25 February 1934 in Shanghai. Her father-in-law, in Wusih, told her to come home; but she did not want to leave Shanghai where her children were in school. After receiving several harsh letters, she and her children took an overdose of veronal on 5 May.

[2] On 20 May a clerk working for a Shanghai chemist committed suicide. A cutting of the report of Mrs. Qin's death was found beside him.

Quite clearly, her suicide shows weakness. But what made her weak? It is important for us to read the letters her worthy father-in-law wrote telling her to go home, in which he urged the good name of their two families and the wishes of the dead conveyed through a planchette. We should also look at the couplet her younger brother wrote for the funeral: 'The wife followed her husband to the grave, the children their mother. . . .' Surely this was written for the admiration of posterity? How could a woman born and bred in such a family avoid being weak? We certainly can blame her for not putting up a struggle; but the all-devouring power of darkness is often too much for a single warrior and those critics of her suicide would not necessarily have helped her in her struggle, for while others are fighting, struggling, and being defeated, they all remain silent. There is no end to the orphans and widows, poor women, and destitute in the by-ways of the countryside or in our great cities and towns, who accept their fate and die, or who struggle against their fate yet eventually perish—but who tells their story, whose heart is touched by them? Truly, they may 'strangle themselves in some ditch or drain, and no one hears of it'.[1]

Men should indeed live—in order to make progress. They should not mind suffering either—in order to put an end to all future suffering. Still more should they fight, but only for reforms. Those who blame another for committing suicide should, at the same time as they blame her, challenge and attack the circumstances which drove her to suicide. If they say not a word and loose not an arrow against the powers of darkness, but simply rail at the 'weak', then no matter how fine-sounding their sentiments, I am forced to say—I can no longer keep silent—that they are simply accomplices of the murderers.

24 May 1934

[1] A quotation from *The Analects*.

Hung by the Heels   倒   提

Because kind-hearted Westerners hate seeing cruelty to animals, anyone who carries hens or ducks upside-down in the International Settlement is penalized. The penalty is merely a fine, and if you are willing to pay you can go on as before. Still, you have been penalized. This has roused the indignation of certain of our compatriots, who say the Westerners are kind to animals but cruel to Chinese, ranking us even lower than poultry.

But this is to misunderstand the Westerners. They despise us, true, but not as lower than beasts. Of course hens and ducks, come what may, end up in the kitchen to be dressed for the table; and even if you carry them the right way up that cannot make amends for their ultimate fate. But since they can neither speak nor resist, what does it profit us to treat them cruelly? The Westerners consider profit in everything. Our ancients were concerned over the suffering caused the people by 'hanging them by the heels' and—what's more—described this graphically, though they never realized how fowl dislike being carried upside down. Attacks were written long ago, however, on the futile torture of 'carving live donkeys' and 'roasting live geese'. Such views are common to both East and West.

But apparently views on men vary. Men can organize themselves and revolt. They can be slaves or masters. If they refuse to exert themselves, they may remain coolies for ever; but if they liberate themselves, they may win equality. It is not necessarily their fate to end up in the kitchen to be dressed for the table. The lower they are, the more their masters pity them. Hence the foreigners' servants who beat dogs are reprimanded, while ordinary people are blamed for being rough with the

servants of foreigners. There is no rule against cruelty to
Chinese in the International Settlement precisely because we
should be able to look after ourselves—we are not hens and
ducks.

But we are so used to that twaddle in the classics about
benevolent champions of justice who free the people from hanging by their heels that even today we keep hoping some little
miracle may drop down from heaven or from some distant
height. 'Better a dog's life in time of peace than a man's in time
of unrest.' We would rather change into dogs than band
together to better our condition. The complaints that we are
worse off than poultry in the International Settlement smack
strongly of this.

Once many men think this way, we shall all be hung by the
heels. And even when we are being sent to the kitchen, no one
will attempt to save us. That is because we are men after all,
but men without guts, without backbone.

3 June 1934

Have the Chinese Lost Their Self-Confidence?

中国人失掉自信力了吗

Judging by published writings it is a fact that two years ago we were constantly boasting of our 'great territory and rich resources'. It is also a fact that before long we stopped boasting, but set our hopes on the League of Nations. And again it is a fact that today we neither boast about ourselves nor have faith in the League of Nations, but have taken to praying to the gods and worshipping Buddha or indulging in nostalgic reminiscences.

So we find people lamenting: the Chinese have lost their self-confidence.

If we go by these few phenomena alone, we lost our self-confidence long ago. Even when we had confidence first in 'territory' and 'resources', then in the 'League of Nations', we had no confidence in 'ourselves'. If that counted as 'confidence' of a kind, all we can say is that the Chinese once had 'confidence in other things', but this has been lost since we were disappointed by the League of Nations.

When a man loses confidence in other things, he has doubts; but he may come round to having faith in himself alone, and this would be a new path. The pity is that we are growing more mystical. Confidence in 'territory' and 'resources' is something palpable; the League of Nations is more nebulous, but at least it does not take long to discover its unreliability. When a man starts praying to the gods and worshipping Buddha, this is so mystical that he cannot quickly discover whether it does good or harm; hence this leads to a longer period of befuddlement.

Now the Chinese are developing 'self-deception'.

'Self-deception' is nothing new either, only now it is daily becoming more evident and all-embracing. But under this cloak we still have Chinese who have not lost their self-confidence.

Since ancient times we have had men who worked doggedly in silence, men who worked stubbornly at the risk of their lives, who strove to save others, who braved death to seek the truth. ... Even the standard dynastic histories, which are really family records of emperors, princes, ministers, and generals, cannot conceal their glory: these men are the backbone of China.

Even now there are many such men. They have firm convictions and do not deceive themselves. When one in front falls others behind fight on. It is only because they are trampled on, kept out of the news, smothered in darkness, that most people have no means of knowing of them. To say that some Chinese have lost their self-confidence is correct, but to say this of the whole nation is downright slander.

In considering the Chinese people, we must not be deceived by the veneer of self-deception but must look at the sinews and backbone. Whether self-confidence exists or not cannot be seen from the writings of scholars and ministers—to find it we have to look underground.

25 September 1934

Tragedies Almost Devoid of Incident

几 乎 无 事 的 悲 剧

The name of Nikolai Gogol is little by little becoming known to Chinese readers, while half of the first part of his master-piece *Dead Souls* has appeared in translation. Though the translation is unsatisfactory, at least it shows us five different types of landowner between chapter 2 and chapter 6, and despite a rich vein of satire, each, with the exception of one old woman and the miser Plushkin, has some sympathetic trait. His serfs, on the other hand, have nothing to recommend them. Even when they are sincerely trying to help the gentry, they do no good, but harm. Gogol himself was a landlord.

Still, the gentry of the time were incensed and launched their usual attacks, alleging that Gogol was the model of most of the types in the novel and that he knew nothing about the land-lords of Russia. This is possible, for the author was a Ukrainian, and judging by his letters home he held views very similar to those of the landlords in the book. But even if he did not under-stand the landlords of Greater Russia, the characters he created are extraordinarily lifelike. Even today, in a different age and country, they still make us feel as if we are meeting old acquain-tances. I shall not speak here of Gogol's brilliant use of satire, but simply of his distinctive method of utilizing ordinary incidents and ordinary conversation to bring out in a most penetrating way the futile existence of the landlords of his time. For example, Nozdrev in chapter 4 is a rascally landlord who is out for pleasure, gambles, tells lies, and demands flattery—but he can take a beating too. Meeting Chichikov in an inn he boasts of his puppy and, having made Chichikov feel its ears, urges him to feel its nose too.

To humour him, Chichikov did as he requested, remarking:
'Yes, he should turn out a fine dog.'

'And feel how cold his nose is! Just take it in your hand!'

Not wanting to offend him, Chichikov felt the puppy's nose and
said: 'This isn't an ordinary nose.'

Even today these boisterous, boastful hosts and smooth-
tongued, worldly guests can be met with everywhere. Some men
even make these their life-long tactics in social intercourse.
'Not an ordinary nose'—what sort of nose is it then? That is
hard to say, but the hearer is satisfied with such an answer.
Later Chichikov goes with Nozdrev to his estate and is shown
all his land and possessions.

Next they looked at a Crimean bitch, already blind and according
to Nozdrev fast approaching her end. Two years ago she had been
a magnificent dog. The party examined the bitch, and it seemed she
really was blind.

Nozdrev is not lying. He boasts of his blind bitch, and it
seems she really is blind. Of what possible interest could this
be to others? Yet there are people who shout, sing praises, and
boast of similar things, doing their utmost to prove them. And
so they spend their whole lives, and pass for busy and honest
men.

These extremely commonplace tragedies, some of them
almost entirely devoid of incident, like speech without words,
are hard to detect unless described by poets. Yet few men perish
in heroic, remarkable tragedies, whereas many fritter their
lives away in extremely commonplace tragedies almost
entirely devoid of incident.

I hear that in Gogol's country what he called 'tearful
smiles' are no longer of any use, their place having been taken
by healthy laughter. In other lands, however, they still come in
useful, for they reflect the existence of many living men.
Besides, even healthy laughter is depressing from the viewpoint
of those being laughed at. So Gogol's 'tearful smiles' on the
faces of readers whose position is different from his become
healthy laughter too. Herein lies the greatness of *Dead Souls*
and also the author's distress.

14 July 1935

Reply to a Letter from the Trotskyites[1]

答 托 洛 斯 基 派 的 信

1 *The letter*

3 June 1936

Dear Mr. Lu Xun,

After the failure of the 1927 Revolution, instead of withdrawing in order to prepare for a comeback, the Chinese communists took to military adventurism. Abandoning work in the cities, they ordered party members to rise everywhere although the tide of revolution had ebbed, hoping to make Reds out of the peasants to conquer the country. Within seven or eight years hundreds of thousands of brave and useful young people were sacrificed on account of this policy, so that now in the high tide of the nationalist movement there are no revolutionary leaders for the city masses, and the next stage of the revolution has been postponed indefinitely.

Now the Reds' movement to conquer the country has failed. But the Chinese communists who blindly take orders from the Moscow bureaucrats have adopted a 'New Policy'. They have made a *volte-face*, abandoned their class stand, issued new declarations and sent representatives to negotiate with the bureaucrats, politicians, and warlords, including those who slaughtered the masses, in order to form a 'united front' with them. They have put away their own banner and confused the people's minds, making the masses believe that all those bureaucrats, politicians, and executioners are national revolutionaries who will resist Japan too. The result can only be to deliver the revolutionary masses into the hands of those executioners for further slaughter. These shameless acts of betrayal on the part of Stalinists make all Chinese revolutionaries blush for shame.

Now the bourgeois liberals and upper strata of the petty bourgeoisie of Shanghai welcome this 'New Policy' of the Stalinists. And well they may. The traditional prestige of Moscow, the blood shed by the Chinese Reds, and their present strength—what could play better into their hands? But the greater the welcome given to this 'New Policy', the greater damage will be done to the Chinese revolution.

[1] For the background of this letter, see Introduction, p. xi.

Since 1930, under the most difficult conditions, our organization has made unremitting efforts to fight for its ideal. Since the defeat of the Revolution we have opposed the recklessness of the Stalinists and advocated a 'revolutionary democratic struggle'. We believe that since the Revolution failed, we must start all over again from the beginning. We have never ceased to gather together revolutionary cadres to study revolutionary theory, accepting the lessons of defeat to educate revolutionary workers so that during this difficult period of counter-revolution we may lay a firm foundation for the next stage of the revolution. The events of the past few years have proved the correctness of our political line and method of work. We were against the opportunist and reckless policies and bureaucratic party system of the Stalinists. Now we resolutely attack their treacherous 'New Policy'. But precisely because of this we are under fire from all sorts of careerists and party bureaucrats. Is this our good fortune or is it a misfortune?

For the last decade and more, sir, I have admired your scholarship, writing, and moral integrity, for while many thinking men have fallen into the quagmire of individualism, you alone have fought on without respite to express your own outlook. We should count it a great honour to hear your criticism of our political views. I am sending you a few of our recent publications, which I beg you to accept and read. If you are good enough to write a reply, please leave it with Mr. X——. I shall go to his house within three days to fetch it.

With best wishes,

CHEN ——

2 The reply

9 June 1936

Dear Mr. Chen,

I have received your letter and the copies of *Struggle* and *Spark* which you sent me.

I take it that the main drift of your letter is contained in these two points: You consider Stalin and his colleagues bureaucrats, and the proposal of Mao Tsetung and others—'Let all parties unite to resist Japan'—as a betrayal of the cause of revolution.

I certainly find this 'confusing'. For do not all the successes of Stalin's Union of Soviet Socialist Republics show the pitifulness of Trotsky's exile, wanderings, and failure which 'forced' him in his old age to take money from the enemy? His conditions as an exile now must be rather different from conditions in Siberia before the revolution, for at that time I doubt if anyone so much as offered the prisoners a piece of bread. He may not feel so good, though, because now the Soviet Union has triumphed. Facts are stronger than rhetoric; and no one expected such pitiless irony. Your 'theory' is certainly much loftier than that of Mao Tsetung: yours is high in the sky, while his is down-to-earth. But admirable as is such loftiness, it will unfortunately be just the thing welcomed by the Japanese aggressors. Hence I fear that when it drops down from the sky it will land on the filthiest place on earth. Since the Japanese welcome your lofty theories, I cannot help feeling concern for you when I see your well-printed publications. If someone deliberately spreads a malicious rumour to discredit you, accusing you of accepting money for these publications from the Japanese, how are you to clear yourselves? I say this not to retaliate because formerly some of you joined certain others to accuse me of accepting Russian roubles. No, I would not stoop so low, and I do not believe that you could stoop so low as to take money from the Japanese to attack the proposal of Mao Tsetung and others to unite against Japan. No, this you could not do. But I want to warn you that your lofty theory will not be welcomed by the Chinese people, and that your behaviour runs counter to present-day standards of morality. This is all I have to say about your views.

In conclusion, this sudden receipt of a letter and periodicals from you has made me rather uncomfortable. There must be some reason for it. It must be because some of my 'comrades-in-arms' have been accusing me of certain faults. But whatever my faults, I am convinced that my views are quite different from yours. I count it an honour to have as my comrades those who are now doing solid work, treading firmly on the ground, fighting and shedding their blood in the defence of the Chinese people. Excuse me for making this an open reply, but since more than three days have passed you will probably not be going to that address for my answer.

Yours faithfully,

LU XUN

Death   死

While preparing a selection of Käthe Kollwitz's works for publication, I asked Miss Agnes Smedley to write a preface. This struck me as most appropriate because the two of them were good friends. Soon the preface was ready, I had Mr. Mao Dun translate it, and it has now appeared in the Chinese edition. One passage in it reads:

All these years Käthe Kollwitz—who never once used any title conferred on her—has made a great many sketches, pencil and ink drawings, woodcuts and etchings. When we study these, two dominant themes are evident: in her younger days her main theme was revolt, but in her later years it was motherly love, the protective maternal instinct, succour and death. All her works are pervaded by the idea of suffering, of tragedy, and a passionate longing to protect the oppressed.

Once I asked her: 'Why is it that instead of your former theme of revolt you now seem unable to shake off the idea of death?' She answered in tones of anguish: 'It may be because I am growing older every day. . . .'

At that point I stopped to think. I estimated that it must have been in about 1910 that she first took death as her theme, when she was no more than forty-three or -four. I stop to think about it now because of my own age, of course. But a dozen or so years ago, as I recall, I did not have such a feeling about death. No doubt our lives have long been treated so casually as trifles of no consequence that we treat them lightly ourselves, not seriously as Europeans do. Some foreigners say that the Chinese are most afraid of death. But this is not true—actually, most of us die with no clear understanding of the meaning of death.

The general belief in a posthumous existence further strengthens the casual attitude towards death. As everyone knows, we

Chinese believe in ghosts (more recently called 'souls' or
'spirits'); and since there are ghosts, after death we can at least
exist as ghosts if not as men, which is better than nothing. But
the imagined duration of this ghostly existence seems to vary
according to one's wealth. The poor appear to believe that
when they die their souls will pass into another body, an idea
derived from Buddhism. Of course, transmigration in Buddhism is a complicated process, by no means so simple; but
the poor are usually ignorant people who do not know this. That
is why criminals condemned to death often show no fear when
taken to the execution ground, but shout: 'Twenty years from
now I shall be a stout fellow again!' Moreover, according to
popular belief a ghost wears the clothes he had on at the time
of death; and since the poor have no good clothes and cannot
therefore cut a fine figure as ghosts, it is far better for them to be
reborn at once as naked babies. Did you ever see a new-born
infant wearing a beggar's rags or a swimming-suit? No, never.
Very well, then, that is a fresh start. Someone may object: If
you believe in transmigration, in the next existence you may
even be worse off or actually become a beast—what a fearful
thought! But the poor don't seem to think that way. They firmly
believe that they have not committed sins frightful enough to
condemn them to becoming beasts: they have not had the
position, power, or money to commit such sins.

But neither do those men with position, power, and money
believe that they should become beasts. They either turn
Buddhist in order to become saints, or advocate the study of
the Confucian classics and a return to ancient ways in order
to become Confucian sages. Just as in life they expect to be
a privileged class, after death they expect to be exempt from
transmigration. As for those who have a little money, though
they also believe they should be exempt from transmigration,
since they have no high ambitions or lofty plans they just wait
placidly. Round about the age of fifty, they look for a burial
place, buy a coffin, and burn paper money to open a bank
account in the nether regions, expecting their sons and grand-
sons to sacrifice to them every year. This is surely much
pleasanter than life on earth. If I were a ghost now, with filial
descendants in the world of men, I should not have to sell my

articles one by one, or ask the Beixin Publishing House for payment. I could simply lie at ease in my cedarwood or fir coffin, while at every festival and at New Year a fine feast and a pile of banknotes would be placed before me. That would be the life!

Generally speaking, unlike the very rich and great, who are not bound by the laws of the nether regions, the poor would like to be reborn at once, while those comfortably-off would like to remain as ghosts for as long as possible. The comfortably-off are willing to remain ghosts because their life as ghosts (this sounds paradoxical but I can think of no better way of expressing it) is the continuation of their life on earth and they are not yet tired of it. Of course there are rulers in the nether regions who are extremely strict and just; but they will make allowances for these ghosts and accept presents from them too, just like good officials on earth.

Then there are others who are rather casual, who do not think much about death even when they are dying, and I belong to this casual category. Thirty years ago as a medical student I considered the problem of the existence of the soul, but did not know what to conclude. Later I considered whether death was painful or not, and concluded that it varied in different cases. And later still I stopped thinking about the matter and forgot it. During the last ten years I have sometimes written a little about the death of friends, but apparently I never thought of my own. In the last two years I have been ill a great deal and usually for a considerable length of time, which has often reminded me that I am growing older. Of course, I have been constantly reminded of this fact by other writers owing to their friendly or unfriendly concern.

Since last year, whenever I lay on my wicker chair recovering from illness, I would consider what to do when I was well, what articles to write, what books to translate or publish. My plans made, I would conclude: 'All right—but I must hurry.' This sense of urgency, which I never had before, was due to the fact that unconsciously I had remembered my age. But still I never thought directly of 'death'.

Not till my serious illness this year did I start thinking distinctly about death. At first I treated my illness as in the

past, relying on my Japanese doctor, S——. Though not a
specialist in tuberculosis, he is an elderly man with a rich
experience who studied medicine before me, is my senior, and
knows me very well—hence he talks frankly. Of course, however well a doctor knows his patient, he still speaks with a
certain reserve; but at least he warned me two or three times,
though I never paid any attention and did not tell anyone.
Perhaps because things had dragged on so long and my last
attack was so serious, some friends arranged behind my back
to invite an American doctor, D——, to see me. He is the only
Western specialist on tuberculosis in Shanghai. After his
examination, although he complimented me on my typically
Chinese powers of resistance, he also announced that my end
was near, adding that had I been a European I would already
have been in my grave for five years. This verdict moved my
soft-hearted friends to tears. I did not ask him to prescribe for
me, feeling that since he had studied in the West he could
hardly have learned how to prescribe for a patient five years
dead. But Dr. D——'s diagnosis was in fact extremely accurate.
I later had an X-ray photograph made of my chest which very
largely bore out his findings.

Though I did not pay much attention to his announcement,
it has influenced me a little: I spend all the time on my back,
with no energy to talk or read and not enough strength to hold
a newspaper. Since my heart is not yet 'as tranquil as an old
well', I am forced to think, and sometimes I think of death too.
But instead of thinking that 'twenty years from now I shall be
a stout fellow again', or wondering how to prolong my stay in a
cedarwood coffin, my mind dwells on certain trifles before
death. It is only now that I am finally sure that I do not believe
that men turn into ghosts. It occurred to me to write a will,
and I thought: If I were a great nobleman with a huge fortune,
my sons, sons-in-law, and others would have forced me to
write a will long ago; whereas nobody has mentioned it to me.
Still, I may as well leave one. I seem to have thought out quite
a few items for my family, among which were:

1. Don't accept a cent from anyone for the funeral. This does
not apply to old friends.

2. Get the whole thing over quickly, have me buried and be done with it.

3. Do nothing in the way of commemoration.

4. Forget me and live your own lives—if you don't, the more fools you.

5. When the child grows up, if he has no gifts let him take some small job to make a living. On no account let him become a writer or artist in name only.

6. Don't take other people's promises seriously.

7. Have nothing to do with people who injure others but who oppose revenge and advocate tolerance.

There were other items, too, but I have forgotten them. I remember also how during a fever I recalled that when a European is dying there is usually some sort of ceremony in which he asks pardon of others and pardons them. Now I have a great many enemies, and what should my answer be if some modernized person asked me my views on this? After some thought I decided: Let them go on hating me. I shall not forgive a single one of them either.

No such ceremony took place, however, and I did not draw up a will. I simply lay there in silence, struck sometimes by a more pressing thought: if this is dying, it isn't really painful. It may not be quite like this at the end, of course; but still, since this happens only once in a lifetime, I can take it. . . . Later, however, there came a change for the better. And now I am wondering whether this was really the state just before dying: a man really dying may not have such ideas. What it will be like, though, I still do not know.

5 September 1936